DIARY OF

A BOSTON MERCHANT,

1764-1779.

A PAPER READ BY

EDWARD L. PIERCE

BEFORE

𝕿𝖍𝖊 𝕸𝖆𝖘𝖘𝖆𝖈𝖍𝖚𝖘𝖊𝖙𝖙𝖘 𝕳𝖎𝖘𝖙𝖔𝖗𝖎𝖈𝖆𝖑 𝕾𝖔𝖈𝖎𝖊𝖙𝖞,

MARCH 14, 1895.

CAMBRIDGE:
JOHN WILSON AND SON.
𝕌𝕟𝕚𝕧𝕖𝕣𝕤𝕚𝕥𝕪 𝕡𝕣𝕖𝕤𝕤.
1895.

This Society has published journals or letters relative to affairs in Boston covering a part of the period (1764–1779) included in Rowe's Diary, among others: Timothy Newell's Journal, April 19, 1775–March 17, 1776, 4 Collections, I. 261–276; Ezekiel Price's Diary, May 28, 1775–Aug. 17, 1776, Proceedings, November, 1863, 185–262; Letters of John Andrews, Feb. 24, 1772–April 11, 1776, Proceedings, July, 1865, 316–412; Thomas Newell's Diary, Jan. 1, 1773–Dec. 22, 1774; Proceedings, October, 1877, 334–363; Letters of Rev. Andrew Eliot, April 25, 1775–Feb. 19, 1776, Proceedings, September, 1878, 280–306; Benjamin Boardman's Diary, July 31–Nov. 12, 1775, Proceedings, May, 1892, 400–413; and Jabez Fitch, Jr.'s, Diary, Aug. 5–Dec. 13, 1775, Proceedings, May, 1894, 40–91. Other journals and memoirs concerning the period are cited in the "Memorial History of Boston," III. 154, note.

The other printed diaries above referred to cover a briefer period than Rowe's; and their authors, or most of them, have a standpoint different from his. Several of them, like Rowe, have much to say of the weather; but that part of his record is omitted in this summary. Rowe himself, without being an acute observer of men and events, was an intelligent merchant; and while we could wish he had reserved a part of the space which he gave to the ever-recurring names of persons whom he met at dinners and clubs for a record of the opinions they expressed, still there remains much which illustrates the public and social life of Boston at this eventful period.

The purpose of this paper is to call attention to interesting points in the Diary, and to give a general knowledge of its contents, which may perhaps be of service to other investigators of local and general history. I have classified the miscellaneous facts and experiences which the diarist states, submitting also a copy of so much of his record as relates to the contest with Great Britain both before the Revolution and during a considerable part of it. I offer as an excuse, if one is needed, for some incidents and details which have been thought worthy of mention, that the newspapers of the period confine themselves mostly to grave documents, telling us but very little of what was going on in the life of the people.

At the time Rowe's Diary begins, — in September, 1764, — the British government was just putting in force its scheme of taxing the Colonies for the purpose as avowed of "defraying the expenses of defending, protecting, and securing the same." The Sugar Act, which imposed duties not only on sugar and molasses but on other articles hitherto exempt, had been passed the previous spring. Otis's pamphlet on "The Rights of the British Colonies asserted and proved" had been issued. In May and during the summer and autumn, protests against the new policy were being made by the Boston town-meeting and the General Court. The Stamp Act was to follow the Sugar Act in less than a twelvemonth. Rowe's Diary thus opens at the initial stage of the Revolution.

The Diary comprises the period of the imposition of the new and hated taxes, the passage and repeal of the Stamp Act, the Boston massacre, the throwing overboard of the tea, the beginning of civil war at Lexington and Concord, the siege of Boston, the evacuation by the British troops, and the visit of the French fleet to the town. The battle of Bunker Hill occurred during the period included in a lost volume.

Boston was, at the period covered by the Diary, a town of sixteen thousand inhabitants, — about the present population of Northampton, or Quincy, in this State, and Concord, New Hampshire, or Burlington, Vermont.

John Rowe was born in Exeter, England, Nov. 16, 1715, and died in Boston, Feb. 17, 1787. His grandfather Jacob Rowe (though the suggestion has been made that he was a great-uncle) held in Exeter the offices of steward, receiver, sheriff, and mayor, holding the last-named office in 1712. Jacob and John Rowe, brothers, emigrated to America, the date of their coming not known; the former going to Quebec, where he became commissary-general, and John coming to Boston. The latter was here as early as 1736, when he was only twenty-one years old, as he purchased that year a warehouse on Long Wharf. This early purchase indicates that he brought considerable means with him; and, besides, he continued to own property in his native city till his death, bequeathing it to his relatives who remained behind. The family is not now traceable in Devonshire.

John Rowe's portrait, at the supposed age of twenty-five, is in the possession of his grand-niece Mrs. Payson, and has been reproduced in F. S. Drake's "Tea Leaves." His costume as there shown is that of a gentleman of the period.

Rowe and his wife were doubtless buried (though no record of interment is preserved) in his vault under the first Trinity Church, a wooden building; and the vault is not supposed to have been disturbed by the subsequent construction of the stone edifice. The vaults were being cleared at the time of the fire of 1872; and the remains found in Rowe's are probably among the "unknown" which were then removed to the Trinity Church tomb in Mt. Auburn Cemetery.

John Rowe was married in 1743 to Hannah Speakman, who survived him eighteen years, dying July 9, 1805, at the age of eighty.[1] Her sister was the first wife of Ralph Inman, the Cambridge Loyalist, with whose family Rowe continued always to be very intimate. The sisters are said to have been twins. Rowe bought in 1764 the estate on the north side of Pond Lane, now Bedford Street, where he lived till his death, and where his widow remained till her death. The year after his purchase he pulled down the house he found standing there on the north side of the lane, and built a new one, into which he moved Oct. 16, 1766. His record of that day is: "Slept this night for this first time in our new house, which is a very good, handsome, and convenient house." Another entry, April 3, 1767, is: "The Governour and his son came to see our new house this afternoon." This house with grounds about it was sold in 1817 by Rowe's heirs to Judge William Prescott;[2] and here he and his son the historian lived. It was demolished in 1845. A picture of it is given in the quarto edition of Ticknor's "Life of William H. Prescott." Rowe owned a considerable tract, measuring nearly three acres, known as "Rowe's Pasture." Without attempting to define its limits accurately, it may be said in a general way that it extended from Bedford Street to Essex Street, with Washington (then Newbury) and Kingston streets as western and eastern limits, not, however, touching Washington Street at any point, and small lots belonging to other people perhaps jutting in here and there. On this ample tract he raised, as his Diary shows, crops of hay and vegetables, and pastured sheep and cattle. He owned houses and lots on the south side of Essex Street as well as in other parts of the town; and one

---

[1] A portrait of Mrs. Rowe is in the possession of Mrs. Charles Amory, Jr., of Boston.

[2] Shurtleff's Topographical and Historical Description of Boston, p. 409.

of his wharves still bears his name. He owned property in other towns, — Dighton, Plymouth, Malden, Medford, Gloucester, Milton, Hardwick, Stoughton, Grafton, Shelburne, Deerfield, and also in Hartford and Woodstock, Connecticut.

Rowe became one of the foremost merchants of Boston. The "Massachusetts Centinel," in noting his death, calls him "an eminent merchant of this place." John Adams[1] names him among the very rich men with whom he had been acquainted in the way of business, placing him among those who had acquired wealth by their own industry, — unlike Hancock, Bowdoin, and Pitts, who had acquired it by descent or marriage. His ships traversed the ocean, and ran along the coast. One of them carried Josiah Quincy, Jr., to Charleston, South Carolina, in February, 1773. His whaling-sloop "Chagford" goes out April 14, 1767; and his sloop "Polly" comes in, Sept. 5, 1771, with 150 barrels of oil. He bought, May 6, 1765, "a cargo of coals of two gentlemen from Newberry." His imported merchandise was miscellaneous, meeting the wants of the people of that day. We get glimpses of what it was here and there. On May 31, 1765, his "warehouse fell in with fish." He dealt largely in salt. On July 3, 1767, a quantity of silk stockings, ribbons, Spanish silk, and Indian and English taffetys were stolen at night from his store. The British troops, when evacuating Boston in March, 1776, took from him "linens, checks, cloths, and woolens," goods of the value of 2260 pounds sterling. Mrs. Commodore Hood visited his store, Dec. 8, 1768, and bought twenty-four yards of superfine silk. A vessel (probably Rowe's) arrives, July 22, 1767, from Madeira with seventy pipes of wine. Governor Hutchinson's accounts[2] show a purchase, July 19, 1770, of Rowe of a quarter cask of port-wine for eight pounds. He was the owner of one of the tea-ships, though in history less is said of his cargo than of Francis Rotch's, which arriving first was the first to be dealt with. Until the conflict between the Colonies and the mother country became one of force, he was largely purveyor for the English fleet, which was rarely absent altogether from the harbor. He was one of the Proprietors of Long Wharf, — that ancient corporation in which leading merchants like Hancock, Winslow, Oliver, Wells, and Boutineau were shareholders. He was also one of the Proprietors of Point Shirley.

[1] Works, ii. 296.   [2] Diary and Letters, i. 77.

Rowe enjoyed excellent health. He makes the entry, Nov. 27, 1773: "This day is my birthday. I am fifty-eight years old. I am at present very hearty and strong, but in my knees rather feeble. I bless God for all his mercies to me"; and again, Nov. 27, 1778: "This day I am sixty-three years old, and I am, thank God, very hearty, though my limbs fail me at times." One of his generous way of living had occasionally need of medical remedies, of which an emetic was the one most frequently resorted to. He records, April 18, 1773: "The doctor has made an apothecary shop in my stomach," — a method of treatment which, in connection with a remedy of his own selection, "a little Geneva of mint," brought the desired relief. He "hurted" his leg, July 25, 1772, on a fishing-excursion. Dr. Heron was his attendant, and, the patient improving too slowly, Dr. Peterson was called in. The doctors were unable "to dry up the wound," and a month after the injury it was "dressed with tincture of myrrh." One record (that of June 13, 14, 1769) gives us reason to prize that then unknown friend of the human race, — anæsthetics: "I went to bed much afflicted with toothache. . . . Sent for Dr. Lloyd to have my tooth drawn; had not resolution to go through the operation."

Mrs. Rowe, like her husband, enjoyed good health. He records, Aug. 4, 1776: "This is Mrs. Rowe's birthday. She is this day fifty-one years old and very hearty and well." She, however, met once (July 15, 1774) with a severe accident in town, when, as she was returning from a funeral, the horses took fright and ran, and, the carriage being upset and herself thrown out, she became unconscious. Her case was thought critical for some days. Dr. Lloyd administered "annidine drops," and he was assisted by Dr. White. Relatives and friends, not hired nurses, watched with the patient. In a week she had much improved; and her husband, whose daily entries speak of her as "my dear, dear Mrs. Rowe," wrote: "She is growing better, for which I and all her friends rejoice." Her husband left her a large part of his property, with full power to dispose of it by will.

Rowe's sentiments in relation to the controversy with Great Britain were those of a moderate, holding in this respect the same position as that of his relatives, intimate friends, and the mass of his fellow-merchants. He was a public-spirited citizen, and wished well to his town and colony, no one more so. He was as strongly opposed as any to the new restrictions on trade which the parent country had put in force, and generally he was not in sympathy with its repressive policy.[1] He served on committees appointed by the town or by merchants to set forth the grievances of the Colony, sometimes willingly and sometimes not so willingly. He was a member of a committee, Sept. 18, 1765 (Otis, chairman), to express the thanks of the town to Conway and Barré for "their noble, generous, and patriotick speeches" in Parliament, and served on similar committees, April 21, 1766, Dec. 4, 1767, and March 14, 1768, — the last being appointed for a recognition of John Dickinson's "Farmer's Letters." He served on a committee, Dec. 18, 1765 (Samuel Adams, chairman), to protest against the shutting up of the courts; on committees, Nov. 20, Dec. 17 and 21, 1767, and June 15 and 17, 1768, to instruct the representatives; on a committee, Oct. 28, 1767, of which he was chairman, to prevent importations, particularly of foreign superfluities, and encourage domestic produce and manufactures; on a large committee, June 14, 1768, to wait on Governor Bernard with a petition for the redress of grievances; and on a committee, September 12 of the same year, to wait on the Governor and inquire as to the reported coming of troops to Boston, and to recommend measures required in the emergency. He signed, Sept. 14, 1768, as one of the selectmen, an address to other towns, protesting against Bernard's dissolving the General Court and against the taxes levied by Parliament. He was chairman of a committee, in June, 1779, to fix the prices of merchandise, and to bring to punishment offenders against the Act prohibiting monopolies and forestalling.[2] As chairman of a merchants' committee, he signed, June 22, 1779, in its behalf a communication to Congress, testifying their patriotic devotion, and reprobating the attempt of "sordid and unprincipled wretches" to depreciate the paper currency by which independence had been almost secured, and "to force a currency of gold and silver on its ruins." This document also expresses "anxiety

---

[1] S. G. Drake, in his "History of Boston," p. 657, states Rowe's signature to a petition to the General Court as early as Dec. 17, 1760, charging the Crown officers with appropriating to their own use money derived from forfeitures.
[2] Independent Chronicle, June 24, 1779.

for the security of that important staple, the fishery," as the main support of the future commerce of the Northern States. Congress, on receiving the petition, passed a resolution of thanks, July 27, 1779, which was communicated to the committee by Elbridge Gerry, James Lovell, and Samuel Holten, then members from Massachusetts.

Rowe, however, while considering the conduct of the British government impolitic and harsh, was indisposed to carry opposition beyond argument, appeal, and protest; and at no time did he favor measures looking to forcible resistance and independence. His position is misconceived when he is classed with the "Patriots," — the party who supported separation from the mother country, and had in view the use of force outside of law to promote that end.[1] Towards Samuel Adams and William Molineux he was not well affected, as his Diary shows. He was, however, prudent enough to keep up pleasant personal relations with both sides. He did not join the patriotic exodus from Boston when the siege began, preferring to remain in order to protect his property.[2] This may have counted against him with the Patriots; for when after the British evacuation he proposed to join in the ceremonies for the interment of Dr. Warren, a brother Mason, he encountered rude treatment from the populace, and found it prudent to withdraw. His close relations with the family of Captain John Linzee, an English navy officer, must have made him an object of suspicion. The popular feeling was, however, soothed in time by his amiable manners, the good offices he freely distributed among his townsmen, his active service on a relief committee, and his general usefulness as a citizen; so that before peace was reached he was elected a representative to the General Court. The looting and pillaging attending the close of the British occupation, in which he was a sufferer, must have sensibly cooled his

[1] This error is found in Frothingham's "Siege of Boston," p. 23; John Adams's Works, ii. 158, note; F. S. Drake's "Tea Leaves," p. 63. Gordon, in his History, i. 209, says Rowe was "a merchant who had been active on the side of liberty in matters of trade," — a statement which, limited to "matters of trade," is true enough. S. G. Drake's "History of Boston," p. 700, note, citing an anonymous memorandum, gives currency to the absurd imputation that Rowe led the mob in the assault on Hutchinson's house. Hutchinson himself may have thought (Diary and Letters, i. 67) that the class of merchants to whom Rowe belonged had stirred up violence against the Crown officers.

[2] He seems, however, to have applied, April 28, 1775, for a pass to go out with his effects, which was for some reason refused.

pounds sterling; and his will, as well as his wife's, provided
liberally for her and her children. Three days after her wedding he records: "Capt. Linzee sailed this forenoon and carried
my dear Sucky with him; I wish them happy together." Absent for nearly three years, they arrived in Boston Easter
Sunday, April 16, 1775, in the "Falcon," which he was then
commanding, bringing with them their first-born, Samuel Hood
Linzee, the future admiral, born Dec. 27, 1773. Rowe brought
the three to his house the same day. Linzee was just in time
to take part in the first armed conflict of the Revolution. On
April 19, 1775, Rowe records: "Capt. Linzee and Capt. Collins in two small armed vessels were ordered to bring off the
troops to Boston, but Lord Percy and Generall Smith thought
proper to encamp on Bunker Hill this night." The fact of
this order has escaped the attention of historians. Linzee had
also on the 20th an engagement with the American troops
below Cambridge bridge.

Mrs. Linzee and her child remained for the next nine months
with Rowe, or with her father then living in town, — her
husband while active on duty being with her from time to time.
He was at Rowe's house at dinner and for the evening on the
day before and the day after the battle of Lexington, and was
there each day till his next sailing, May 1, from Boston; and now
and then till after the siege his presence at Rowe's house is recorded.[1] He commanded, June 19, the "Falcon," one of the six
vessels which cannonaded the American works on Bunker Hill.
He sailed, Jan. 20, 1776, in the "Falcon" for England, taking
his wife, his son, and infant daughter Hannah, born in Boston,
and also his brother-in-law George Inman. Later he commanded
the "Pearl"; and after the war, as commander of the "Penelope," he was in Boston Harbor, Sept. 9, 1790, and applied
to Governor Hancock for permission to enter the harbor with
his ship, offering to fire a salute and expecting one in return.
Hancock's answer is not known, but it was certainly one of consent; for it appears that the "Penelope" sailed from Boston,
September 17, leaving, however, its commander behind, "lying
very dangerously ill of a fever at his house in this town."[2] He

---

[1] Linzee's name appears as being at Rowe's April 17, 18, 20, 21, 22, 23, 24, 25, 26, 27, 28, 29, 30, Dec. 27, 28, 1775; Jan. 2, 7, 11, 14, 1776. Rowe's Diary from May 30, 1775, to Dec. 25, 1775, is missing.

[2] Massachusetts Centinel, Sept. 18, 1790.

in May, 1765, when he failed, receiving 238 votes, — James Otis, who was chosen, receiving 388, and the other successful candidates, Thacher, Cushing, and Gray, a still larger number. At the special election in September, 1765, for filling the vacancy caused by the death of Oxenbridge Thacher, there was no choice on the first ballot, — the vote being Samuel Adams 247, Rowe 137, John Ruddock 110, and John Hancock 40. Adams was chosen on the next ballot, and this was the beginning of his legislative career. The next May, Rowe, who had 309, was defeated by Hancock, who had 437, — Otis, Cushing, and Adams receiving each between six and seven hundred.[1] The story is, as told by Gordon in his History,[2] that Adams promoted the election of Hancock, saying, when Rowe's name was mentioned for the place, and pointing at the same time to Hancock's house, "Is there not another John that may do better?" This piece of gossip, which has been much copied,[3] is quite untrustworthy. It is not unlikely, however, that Adams threw his influence against Rowe, not thinking him earnest enough for the work in hand, or perhaps piqued by his rivalry at the special election. Rowe was again unsuccessful in 1767, when he received only 134 votes; and he was not afterwards a candidate for a considerable period. He was, however, chosen a member for the years 1780-1784. As a member in 1780 (being chosen also at the election in October), he took part in the inauguration of the State Constitution. He failed of a re-election in 1781, when there were several candidates, Samuel Adams heading the list; but Adams, already chosen a Senator, elected to go to the higher chamber, and at a special election (June 12) Rowe received 300 out of 394 votes cast.[4] Why Adams, chosen a Senator a few weeks before, was placed on the Representative ticket, particularly as his subsequent choice between the two offices shows that he did not wish to go to the House, is not easily understood. Rowe as a Representative moved, March 17, 1784, the restoration of the "Cod Fish" to its former place in the State House as the symbol of an important industry. The removal of this relic to the

[1] Drake's "History of Boston," p. 719, is in error in stating Rowe's election at this time.
[2] I. 142.
[3] John Adams's Works, ii. 158, note; Wells's "Life of Samuel Adams," i. 119.
[4] Adams's biographer, Wells, does not refer to this double election, only mentioning his election as Senator.

new legislative chamber, March 7, 1895, has revived his memory.

Rowe was greatly interested in Trinity Church, connecting himself with it somewhere between 1741 and 1744, — probably in 1743, at the time of his marriage, when it was only eight years old.[1] Late in that year he bought pew 82, as appears by the records. His wife's relatives the Speakmans appear to have been connected with it from the first. The subscription list, open from 1741 to 1744 for its organ, bears his name with twenty pounds annexed to it. He was chosen a vestryman in 1760, and continued to be one till his death, except for one or two years (1776–1777), when he was warden. He became a communicant in 1766. He was from the first a generous giver, and for most of the time of his connection with the church he contributed a larger sum to its funds than any one else. He was rarely absent from both Sunday services, except when ill, or troubled in spirit, or the barber failed to come; notes always the text, which he copies at length; follows closely the sermons, which he remarks upon as "very clever," "very elegant," "most excellent," "delightful," "sensible," "serious," "very polite," "pathetic and moving," "metaphysical," or "well delivered." He has much to say of parish affairs, — Mr. Banister's ejectment suit against the church (Dec. 31, 1764; Jan. 2, Feb. 18, March 19, 1765), being appointed (Jan. 6, 1765) on the church committee in relation to it; the cracking of the church's bell (March 6, 1774), which was given a few months later (October 2) to a sister church in Norwich, Conn.; the collections for the poor at Christmas (£400 8s., old tenor, Dec. 25, 1773); the raising of the minister's salary (April 5, 1765); the new organ in 1770 (October 5 and December 9); the proposed alteration of the church (July 26, 1772), as to which he regrets to see the gentlemen so indifferent; the convention of the Episcopal clergy (June 17, 1767); the death of Rev. William Hooper, who expired instantaneously in his garden, April 14, 1767, "to the great grief and sorrow of his people and the loss of his family," whom Rowe calls his own "most valuable and worthy and never to be forgotten friend"; and the contribution of £253 for "good Mrs. Hooper," May 13, 1770. Rowe writes, on the day of the funeral, April 17:

[1] The manuscript records of Trinity Church have assisted in filling out the Diary as to Rowe's connection with it.

"After church returned to the house of mourning, and I endeavored to give comfort to the bereaved family: I intend to be their friend." The only mention of the great Boston artist comes a few days later, in the entry of April 23: "Mrs. Hooper went to Coply's to have her picture drawn, as did Capt. Dalton [of Newberry] and wife."

Rowe was the intimate friend of the successive ministers, Hooper, Walter, Parker, and of their families as well. Their evenings, particularly Sunday evenings, were often passed at his house. He "smoaked a pipe," June 11, 1765, with Mr. Hooper. Mr. Parker, in recognition of his uniform kindness, named a son for him; and Rowe, in recognition of the friendship, bequeathed a legacy to the father and an estate on Pond Lane to the son, his namesake. He was a peacemaker, composing differences between ministers, as when Mr. Walter on one occasion took umbrage at some behavior of Mr. Hooper (July 13, 16, 1765). The clergy would have a sunnier life if all parishioners were as friendly critics of their sermons as was he, — when, for instance, he wrote, Aug. 15, 1773, "Mr. Walter shines more and more in his preaching," and, a week later, "he is so good a man that my pen cannot describe his virtues."

Now and then a stranger clergyman appears. On June 9, 1765, "The Rev Mr. Cooper, President of the Colledge at New York, preached." The record for May 10, 1772, is, "Mr. Thompson of Scituate read prayers and preached [in the morning and the afternoon]. . . . Both these sermons were honestly designed but very lengthy."

Nearly a year after Mr. Hooper's death, April 4, 1768, Rev. William Walter was chosen unanimously his successor,[1] with a salary of 156 pounds sterling, and a gratuity of 50 pounds sterling for the year to Mrs. Hooper.

Rowe took especial interest in the calling of new ministers, and a good voice seems to have been an essential requisite in a candidate. Dec. 7, 1772, "a young gentleman from Andover," who had been recommended for assistant, "read prayers in the church this morning to several of us that we might judge of his voice, and I think he has a pleasant and agreeable voice." Oct. 5, 1773, Rev. Samuel Parker of Portsmouth read several chapters privately in the church to "the gentlemen of the

---

[1] The "Memorial History of Boston," iii. 128, implies an immediate succession. A. H. Chester's "Trinity Church," published in 1888, contains a similar error.

vestry" to show what his voice was. He was found to have "a good voice," and to read "with propriety;" "was much liked," and the wardens and vestry "were all of them for him" as assistant (October 7, 10). He sailed for England, Nov. 6, 1773, for ordination, and arrived home May 16, 1774. Rowe's record for May 22 is that he then "preached for the first time from 123ᵈ Psalm and the 1ˢᵗ verse a sensible, good discourse, and very well delivered for his first time of preaching."

The parting of the ways was at hand. Mr. Parker informed the wardens and vestry, July 18, 1776, that he could not with safety perform the entire service as before, that he was interrupted the previous Lord's Day when reading the prayers for the King, and that he had received threats of interruption and insult in case of a repetition, and was fearful of damage to the church; and he desired counsel and advice. The wardens and vestry decided (the proprietors concurring), as the only alternative for shutting up the church, in view of the temper and spirit of the people, to request the minister to omit the part of the liturgy which related to the King; and Mr. Parker acted accordingly.

Mr. Walter left for England in 1776. The proprietors, April 10, 1776, invested Mr. Parker, the assistant minister, for one year with all the powers of incumbent minister. Three years afterwards they voted, June 13, 1779, after correspondence with Mr. Parker, that "the church has not an incumbent minister, 12 yeas, 4 nays." Two of the proprietors, Colonel Hatch and Mr. Bethune, withdrew before the vote. A week later Mr. Parker was chosen incumbent minister at a salary of three pounds sterling a week; and after some reflection on the propriety of taking the place in view of his friendly relations with Mr. Walter, he accepted, July 25.[1] Some idea of the condition of the church shortly after the siege had ended may be had from Rowe's entry May 26, 1776: "Mr. Parker preached a well adapted and good discourse. I staid at the sacrament this day, about fifty communicants." The proprietors of King's Chapel proposed, April 4, 1776, in view of the financial difficulty in keeping both churches open, a united service at the Chapel for both churches, with Mr. Parker as the

---

[1] The "Memorial History of Boston," iii. 129, says that "Mr. Parker became rector soon after the war," which is not strictly correct. A. H. Chester's "Trinity Church," p. 11, has the same error.

minister; but Trinity Church (Rowe being chairman of the committee) declined to suspend their own services.

Rowe, while a loyal Episcopalian, was observant of what was going on in other denominations, sometimes attending their special services, as the installation of Rev. Samuel Blair, in Dr. Sewall's Meeting House, Nov. 19, 1766, where Mr. Pemberton prayed and Mr. Blair preached; the ordination of Rev. Simeon Howard at the West Church, May 6, 1767, where Dr. Chauncy preached, and "before and after the ceremony there was an anthem sung"; the preaching of an Indian minister, Mr. Oatum (Aug. 22, 1773), at Mr. Moorhead's, the Presbyterian church in Long Lane, afterwards Federal Street; the election sermon of Rev. Mr. Shute of Hingham (May 25, 1768),—"a very long sermon, being an hour and forty minutes." The entry July 9, 1766, is: "This morning about five of clock the Rev⁴ Dr. Mayhew died much lamented by great numbers of people." These seem to have been the best days of the Quakers in Boston, who had had a place of worship in the town for more than a hundred years. Rowe notes, July 21, 1769: "This afternoon Mrs. Rachel Willson, the famous Quaker preacher, preached in Faneuil Hall to at least twelve hundred people; she seems to be a woman of good understanding."

A very interesting religious event of this period in Massachusetts was the visit of the most renowned evangelist of modern times, George Whitefield. These were his last days; he was to sleep in the land he loved so well; and his sepulchre is where his voice was last heard calling sinners to repentance. He came to us in the midst of great excitement on public affairs; and it is pleasant to think of him that our fathers had his sympathies, and that in the last letter he is known to have written, just a week before his death, he said feelingly: "Poor New England is much to be pitied, Boston most of all. How falsely misrepresented!" Whitefield came from Wrentham to Boston Aug. 14, 1770. He preached at the old North Church the 15th, at Dr. Sewall's the 16th, at Dr. Eliot's the 17th, at Mr. Pemberton's the 18th, at the New North (Dr. Eliot's) the 20th, at Dr. Sewall's the 21st and 22d, at the New North the 23d, at Dr. Sewall's the 24th, at Cambridge the 27th, at Charlestown the 28th,[1] at the Old South the 29th, at the New

[1] Tyerman's "Life of Whitefield," ii. 502, reverses the dates at Cambridge and Charlestown.

North the 30th, at Jamaica Plain the 31st, at Milton September 1st, at Roxbury the 2d, at the Old South the 3d; and on the 4th he set out for Portsmouth. The Diary does not give a record of services on August 19th, 25th, and 26th.[1] Rowe heard him twice, on August 16th and 24th, and notes the text on both occasions, saying of the first sermon (text Zechariah ix. 12, 1st clause), "I liked his discourse," and of the second (text St. Matthew xxii. 11–13), "This was in my opinion a clever discourse." His entry Sunday, September 30, is, "The Rev⁴ Mr. Whitfield died suddenly this morning at Newberry, much lamented." His death was at 6 A. M., probably of *angina pectoris;* and a special messenger must have been despatched to carry the intelligence to Boston.[2]

Among the pageants of the town, funeral ceremonies were the foremost. Those of eminent clergymen and lawyers and of civil or military officers drew a multitude of spectators. Rev. Dr. Mayhew was buried July 11, 1766, — a day when the thermometer stood at 90°. Besides a long procession of men and women on foot, preceding and following the remains, were fifty-seven carriages, of which sixteen were coaches and chariots, — Dr. Chauncy making the prayer and many clergymen attending. Similar rites accompanied, April 17, 1767, "the mournful funeral of Rowe's worthy and much lamented friend," Rev. Mr. Hooper, with "a great concourse and multitude of people attending the solemnity hardly to be conceived, . . . so great at the [Trinity] church that a great many gentlemen and ladies could not get in. . . . Rev⁴ Mr. Walter preached a very pathetick and moving discourse." "A great concourse of people attended the funeral" of the Rev. Mr. Moorhead, Dec. 6, 1773. The funerals of Captain Hay of the warship "Tamar," March 23, 1773, and particularly of Lieutenant-Governor Andrew Oliver, March 8, 1774, combined civic and military pomp, — coaches, chariots, solemn music, Hancock and his Cadets, the

---

[1] His biographer, Tyerman (ii. 592), says that he preached at Malden the 19th and at Medford on the 26th. Neither he nor the Boston newspapers take note specially of his preaching on the 25th.

[2] Some of the clergymen were not well affected towards Whitefield's theology and methods. This was the case with Rev. Nathaniel Robbins of Milton, who refused to admit Whitefield to his church; and the latter preached in the open air on Milton Hill, in front of the house which was the former home of William Foye, provincial treasurer, under an elm which stood till the storm of 1851. Teele's "History of Milton," pp. 116, 117.

firing of minute-guns, and the presence of officials of high rank. Henry Vassall's funeral at Cambridge, March 22, 1769, is described as "a very handsome funeral and a great number of people and carriages." But the most august rites in honor of the dead accompanied, Sept. 12, 1767, the burial of Jeremiah Gridley, the great lawyer of the Province, father of the bar of Boston, master and guide of John Adams in legal studies, Grand Master of the Masons (Rowe being then Deputy Grand Master). Preceding the remains were the officers of his regiment and one hundred and sixty-one Masons in full regalia and bearing the symbols of the order; and following them were the Lieutenant-Governor, the judges and James Otis as bearers, then relatives, lawyers in their robes, gentlemen of the town, a great many coaches, chariots, and chaises, with "such a multitude of spectators as Rowe had never before seen since he had been in New England." After the interment the procession returned in the same order to the Town House, whence the body had been taken at the beginning. Rowe remarks of the display: "I do not much approve of such parade and show; but as it was his and his relations' desire, I could not well avoid giving my consent."

Notwithstanding the Act of 1750 prohibiting "stage plays and other theatrical entertainments," our fathers found ways of amusing themselves with public exhibitions which sometimes came almost if not quite within the statute. There was, Oct. 26, 1764, an afternoon "show at the White Horse which was a very faint representation of the city of Jerusalem; in short tis a great imposition on the publick." March 13, 1765, Rowe "went in the evening over to Gardner's to see the Orphan acted, which was miserably performed, about 210 persons there." Sept. 15, 1767, he "spent the evening at Blodget's in seeing Hinds, the ballance master, perform; he is but a clumsy hand." March 23, 1770, he "went in the evening to the Concert Hall to hear Mr. Joan read the Beggars Opera and sing the songs; he read but indifferently, but sung in taste; there were upwards one hundred people there." The legal restrictions imposed by a Puritan State were suspended during the British occupation. These are some of Rowe's notes: Dec. 29, 1775, "The Busy Body acted tonight"; Jan. 22, 1776, "This evening the tragedy of Tamerlane, to which was added the Blockade of Boston,[1] was performed at Faneuil Hall"; Feb. 24, 1776, "Last evening the Wonder of Wonders was acted and generally approved off."

The town was not without musical entertainments. Jan. 5, 1768, at Joseph Harrison's in the evening, "Mr. Mills of New Haven entertained us most agreeably on his violin; I think he plays the best of any performer I ever heard." March 16, 1769, "Spent the evening at the Fife Major's concert at Concert Hall; there was a large and genteel company and the best musick I have heard performed there." Jan. 3, 1771, "Spent the evening at Concert Hall, where there was a concert performed by Hartly Morgan and others; after the concert a dance. The Commodore and all the captains of the navy here was there, and Colo. Dalrymple, and fifty or sixty gentlemen and the same number of ladies present." Feb. 8, 1771, " Mr Morgan, the fidler, had a benefit concert tonight." Oct. 15, 1771, "I spent the former part of the evening at the Concert Hall, it being Mr. Propert's concert; a good company, upwards of 200." The same person, who was the organist at Trinity Church, gave three concerts at the Coffee House, March 3, 17, 31, 1773, with "good music" bebefore "a very genteel company." March 15, 1771, Mr. Propert at Rowe's House "diverted us all the evening by playing on Sucky's [Inman's] spinnet and joyned by Mr. J. Lane in singing; Propert is a fine hand." Two other diversions may be noted here. At a tavern, Jan. 22, 1767, "a stranger diverted us much in playing the slight of hand." At Rowe's house, Jan. 29, 1770, " Mr. J. Lane read us the diverting farce, the Mayor of Garratt." It was before the days of Gall and Spurzheim; but, July 31, 1769, " In the evening I went to hear Mr. Douglass lecture on heads; he performed well."

There were feats of horsemanship, precursors of the modern circus. Nov. 1, 1771, "After dinner we went over to Bracket's and see a Yorkshire man stand upon a horse's back and gallop him full speed, afterwards upon two horses, and after that on three; he endeavored to make all them gallop as fast as he could; then he mounted a single horse and run him full speed, and while running he jumped off and on three several times." Sept. 8, Oct. 5, 12, 1773, there were other like performances by Mr.

[1] Washington was travestied in this performance.

tridges, the first of the season (Aug. 30, 1766); fresh cod (March 5, 1765), "turtogue" (Sept. 4, 1767), and fresh-water fish, — trout, pike, and perch, often very large, and caught by Rowe himself. The only vegetable named is green peas, picked from his own garden (June 16, 1767). Of the fruits which now complete a dinner or give relish to a breakfast or tea, nothing is said except that at Inman's one afternoon (July 6, 1768) there was at tea "a fine desert of cherrys and strawberries," the last doubtless growing wild. "A good large plumb cake" accompanied, June 5, 1769, "a fine ball and excellent music in Faneuil Hall."

The Diary suggests the beverages of the time. Then, as in more modern periods, Boston people delighted in Old Madeira. Hutchinson, in his almanac for 1770, notes: "July 19, paid John Rowe for a qr. cask of Port, £8." At a dinner at Rowe's, July 5, 1765, "Christo. Minot was very wroth with Mr. Inman for introducing some sterlg. Madeira on his new coat from one of the Leghorn glasses not well managed." May 1, 1766, "After dinner came Capt. Solo. Davis and Mr. H. Bethune to drink Welch ale." At the dinner on the Queen's birthday at Concert Hall (Jan. 18, 1771) there was "very good dancing and good musick, but very bad wine and punch." At Mrs. Cordis's tavern (March 25, 1767) her patrons "regulated the price of wine and punch with her, twenty shillings a double bowl punch, thirty shillings a bottle Madeira." March 7, 1767, "we went to Capt. Bennets and drank a bottle of Madeira with Lewis Gray and Capt. Doble."

The private dinners at which Rowe was host or guest bring before us the principal citizens of Boston at that time. One misses altogether, in the repeated lists of names, Paul Revere, not then ranking with people of social consideration, and finds only in a very few instances Samuel Adams sharing in the conviviality. The last-named, with Hancock and Cushing, dines with Rowe May 5, 1767, and again Feb. 15, 1774, in company with Colonel James Warren of Plymouth, and other guests, not of Boston, bearing military titles. Rowe meets Adams at a dinner at Henderson Inches's, Jan. 7, 1775, in company with the clergymen Hunt and Bacon, Ezekiel Goldthwait, Cushing, and Arnold Wells. Otherwise Samuel Adams is not traced at dinners and clubs, except at the Fire Club.

Rowe's relations as friend and client with John Adams seem

tain Thomas Gerry of Marblehead (Sept. 18, 1769), and his son Elbridge, then rising to distinction (May 26, 1767; June 29, 1770); Robert Treat Paine of Taunton (Feb. 8, March 1, 1767); Colonel John Chandler of Worcester and Colonel John Murray of Rutland (March 1, June 8, 10, 1767; Dec. 8, 5, 1769); and General Timothy Ruggles of Hardwick (March 1, 1767). He had (Sunday, Jan. 10, 1768) General Winslow of Marshfield to dine with him; and after church he spent an hour at Mrs. Bracket's, the tavern, with General Winslow, General Ruggles, Colonel Bradford, Mr. Sever of Kingston, and Major Alden.

Occasionally there were guests from other Colonies, — an Izzard, Burrows, and Powell from South Carolina, or a Livingston, King, and Mercer from New York (July 15, Aug. 21, 1767; Aug. 6, 7, 8, Sept. 6, 7, Oct. 15, 19, 21, 23, 1776); visitors or traders from the West Indies (Aug. 27, 1772; Sept. 6, 1776); Mr. Conner of Madeira and Mr. Conner of Teneriffe (Nov. 16, 1772); occasionally Frenchmen and Spaniards (July 16, 1772); and Englishmen who came for trade or curiosity (Oct. 12, Nov. 23, 1772), now and then bearing titles, as for instance Lord and Lady William Campbell (Oct. 25, 30, 1771; July 4, 1772). The English officers, civil and military, were much in social request; and some of them had to seek Rowe's good offices to relieve them from arrest for debt or other difficulties, as in the cases of Sir Thomas Rich of the "Senegal" (Nov. 7, 1771), and Captain John Linzee (Aug. 26, 27, 28, 31, 1772). Rowe often notes the sailing or arrival of passengers, both English and American, to or from England; and there seems to have been more communication between the town and the mother country than between the town and the Colonies lying southward. It is thus easy to understand how Boston at an early day acquired a distinctively English stamp.

A romantic character appears transiently in Rowe's pages, — Lady Frankland, born Agnes Surriage in 1726, the Marblehead girl, celebrated in Holmes's ballad, who attracted the eye of Sir Charles Henry Frankland, great-grandson of Frances Cromwell, the daughter of the Protector.[1] He had come to Boston

[1] Sir Charles Henry Frankland, by Elias Nason; Foote's Annals of King's Chapel, i. 515-518. Frankland did not come to his title till the death of his uncle in 1747. His memorandum book or journal is preserved in the cabinet of this Society.

as royal collector in 1741. Though closely identified with
King's Chapel as vestryman in the years 1743-44 and 1746-54,
he was a benefactor of Trinity Church, giving, as appears by
its records, a subscription for its first organ which was exceeded
only by the amounts contributed by Peter Faneuil and Henry
Vassall. Besides his city house next to Hutchinson's,[1] he
bought, as is well known, an estate in Hopkinton, now Ashland,
where he placed his mistress, whom several years afterwards
he married at Lisbon, in gratitude for her having rescued him
at the time of the earthquake in 1755. Sir Henry and Lady
Frankland were again in Boston in 1756, and they entertained
the Rowes and Inmans Jan. 26, 1757. They left the country
Feb. 23, 1758.

Once or twice more Frankland came to Boston, and returning to England died near Bath, Jan. 11, 1768. He was
accompanied by Henry Cromwell, said to be his natural son,
born in February, 1741, before his acquaintance with the
Marblehead girl whom he took with him to Boston and
Hopkinton. A few months after her husband's death Lady
Frankland and Henry Cromwell sailed for Boston. Rowe's
entries concerning them are: June 8, 1768. "Capt. Free-
man arrived from Bristol, in whom came passengers Lady
Frankland and Henry Cromwell." June 9. "Dined at home
with Mr. Henry Cromwell, Lady Frankland, Mr. Inman,
Capt. Solo. Davis, Mrs. Rowe, and Sucky. After dinner
Mr. Harrison and Mrs. Harrison paid us a visit, spent the
evening at home with the same company." July 6. "After
dinner Mr. James Otis and myself went to Mr. Inman's,
where we found Colo. Phipps and wife, Mr. John Apthorp
and wife, Capt. Solo. Davis and wife, Mr. Cromwell and Lady
Frankland," and others. July 7. "Dined at Colo. David
Phipps at Cambridge, with him and wife, Mr. John Apthorp
and wife, Mr. William Davis and wife, Mr. Henry Cromwell,
Mr. Inman, Lady Frankland," and others. July 9. "Dined at
Ten Hills with Mr. Robt. Temple and wife, Mr. Cromwell,
Lady Frankland, Mr. Stewart, Mr. Fenton, Mrs. Fenton,
Mr. Inman, Mrs. Inman, Mrs. Rowe, Miss Bessy Temple
and Mr. Temple's 4 daughters; in the afternoon we were
joyned by Mr. John Temple, the surveyor and lady." July

[1] Memorial History of Boston, ii. 525-527, where a picture of the house is
given.

26. "Spent the afternoon with Lady Frankland, Mrs. McNeal, Mrs. Wᵐ Gould, Mrs. Rowe, and Sucky." July 28. "Dined at home with Capt. Joseph Williams, Mr. Henry Cromwell, Mr. Tristram Dalton, Mr. Inman, Mrs. Rowe, Sucky, and George Inman." August 24. "Spent the evening at Lady Frankland's with her and her sister, Mr. Cromwell, Madam Apthorp, Dr. Bulfinch, Mrs. Bulfinch, Mr. Inman, Mrs. Rowe, and Sucky." August 30. "Dined at Mr. Laviount's at Cambridge with him and Mrs. Laviount, Mr. Cromwell and Lady Frankland," the rest being Sheaffes, Phippses, Apthorps, Greenleafs, Davises, and Inmans. Rowe meets Cromwell September 16 and November 1 in large companies. November 9. "Spent the remainder [of the evening] at home with Mr. Inman, Mr. Cromwell, Lady Frankland, her sister, Mrs. Rowe, and Sucky." December 1. "Spent the evening at Capt. Solomon Davis, with him, Mrs. Davis, . . . Lady Frankland, Mr. Cromwell," and others. March 22, 1769. "Dined at Mr. Inman's at Cambridge with him, Mr. Cromwell, Lady Frankland," and others. Lady Frankland and Cromwell were of a party at Menotomy Pond Aug. 28, 1773; and they disappear at this date from Rowe's Diary. Lady Frankland probably left shortly after for her estate in Hopkinton. She and Cromwell remained there till 1775, when after some obstruction they were allowed by the Provincial Congress to go to Boston, and not long after sailed for England, never to return.[1] The curious history of Agnes Surriage is only pursued thus far in order to illustrate Rowe's Diary. It may be added that she married in 1782 John Drew, a banker of Chichester, and died, April 23, 1783, at the age of fifty-seven. The only glimpses of her sojourn in Boston after her return as a widow are now for the first time obtained from Rowe's Diary.

Henry Cromwell's origin is involved in obscurity. Sir Charles Henry Frankland is usually named as his putative father, but the history which comes nearest the time makes him the natural son of Sir Thomas Frankland, Sir Charles's uncle and immediate predecessor in the title.[2] No writer makes any suggestion as to his maternity. He entered the English navy, rose to be a captain, and was with Admiral Kempenfelt in an action off the

---

[1] Memorial History of Boston, iii. 77.
[2] Noble's Memoirs of the House of Cromwell, ii. 423, 424. Noble makes two mistakes, — giving Agnes's name as "Brown," and giving "Colchester" instead of Chichester as the place where she passed the latter part of her life.

French coast Nov. 14, 1781. He is said to have been living and to have had a family in Chichester in 1796. Nason makes a statement which is not trustworthy,—that, "being unwilling to fight against his native country, he retired from the service previous to the close of the Revolution." There is no evidence of his American birth, and the dates indicate an English birth. It appears by Steel's "List of the Royal Navy," page 20, that his first commission was in 1781, and that, instead of leaving the navy, he was still in it in 1797, with the rank of captain.

Weddings were the occasion of good cheer and gayety. Rowe mentions, Nov. 8, 1764, "Mr. Thos. Amory married Miss Betty Coffin this evening; there was a great company at old Mr. Coffin's on the occasion, and a great dance."[1] He records, Jan. 13, 1767, "a wedding frollick" at John Erving, Jr.'s, where he "had the pleasure to dance with the bride." Feb. 2, 1768. "This morning Miss Polly Hooper was married in Trinity Church to Mr. John Russell Spence by the Rev^d Mr. Walter; a great concourse of people attended on the occasion. Dined at Mrs. Hooper's with her, the new bridegroom and bride." A large number of guests were present,—Hallowells, Apthorps, Murrays, Greenleafs, and others,—remaining to tea and joining in the evening in a dance. "We were merry, and spent the whole day very clever and agreeable."

There were once in two weeks in the winter and spring, beginning with the first of January, dancing-assemblies at Concert Hall. The Governor and military and naval officers quite often attended them, and Rowe describes them many times as "very brilliant." The number of gentlemen and ladies in attendance was usually rather more than a hundred, and sometimes it rose to two hundred. Feb. 10, 1768. "Spent the evening at the assembly, which was a very brilliant one, the Governour and Lady, all the commissioners, Mr. Harrison, and too many to enumerate." March 15, 1769. "Spent the evening at the assembly with the Governour, Commodore, General, Colo. Kerr, Colo. Lesly, Major Furlong, Major Fleming, Major Fordyce, a great number of officers of the navy and army and gentlemen and ladies of the town, that is, was a brilliant assembly and very good dancing." Other assembly

[1] The bride's portrait belongs to the family of the late William Amory of Boston.

evenings are noted March 1, 29, April 12, 1769; Jan. 4, 18, Feb. 1, March 14, May 3, June 4, 1771; Jan. 2, 30, 1772; Jan. 18, 1773.

There were several political clubs in Boston in Rowe's time, but he belonged to none of them. He was however an habitual visitor at clubs social or commercial, going almost every evening to one or another. More often than any other he sought the "Possee"; but what was its bond of fellowship is not known. It had a limited number of members, as follows: John Avery, John Box, William Coffin Senior, Samuel Deming, Deacon Thomas Foster, Benjamin Greene, Rufus Greene, William Henshaw, Francis Johonnot, James Richardson, and John Rowe. Samuel Swift, the lawyer, usually met with them, though perhaps rather as a guest than as a member. Occasionally a member introduced a guest who lived in the country.

The Fire Club, meeting at Mrs. Cordis's or at Ingersoll's, was made up of George Bethune, Melatiah Bourne, James Boutineau, Nicholas and Thomas Boylston, John Brown, John Dennie, Solomon Davis, Benjamin Faneuil, Samuel Fitch, Thomas Flucker, Harrison Gray, Capt. Jerry Green, Joseph Green, Dr. William Lloyd, Master John Lovell, William Molineux, and William Sheaffe. Rowe's first meeting with them was Sept. 5, 1768. On the same page where he states this fact he writes, "The word, Ask more," which may have been the password. Joseph Green, who was present Sept. 4, 1769, is mentioned as "the poet."

Rowe attended, Nov. 7, 14, 1764, the Wednesday Night Club, probably having no connection with the Wednesday Evening Club of a later date. He also mentions, July 4, 1767, meeting the "No. 5 Club," made up of prominent citizens whom he names.

The chief rendezvous of the leading citizens was, however, at Mrs. Cordis's,— "the British Coffee House in the front room towards the Long wharf where the Merchants Club has met this twenty years."[1] Lawyers as well as merchants came hither, probably every evening. In 1767 the meetings were at Mrs. Cordis's; but about 1772 they were held at Colonel Joseph Ingersoll's Bunch of Grapes in King Street, and when he left Boston, at Captain Marston's, either in King Street or

[1] John Adams's Diary, Works, ii. 200.

Merchants' Row. The names of persons whom Rowe met at these resorts — some on one evening and some on another, and all of them recurring again and again in his pages — are John Amiel, George Apthorp, Nat. and George Bethune, Joshua Blanchard, Melatiah and William Bourne, James Boutineau, John and Nicholas Boylston, Thomas Brattle, Edward, Solomon, and William Davis, John Dennie, Joseph Dowse, John Erving, Samuel Fitch, Thomas Flucker, Ezekiel Goldthwait, Thomas Gray, Treasurer Harrison Gray, John Hancock, Samuel Hughes, Nat. Hide, Henderson Inches, Joseph Jackson, William Molineux, James Otis, Edward Payne, James Perkins, Dr. William Lee Perkins, Samuel Quincy, Joseph Scott, John Timmins, James Warden, Edward Wendell, and Joshua Winslow, and the lawyers Gridley, Sewall, and Swift.

The habit of frequenting insurance offices for reading newspapers and hearing gossip belongs to a later date; but Rowe records, Aug. 22, 1768: "Spent the evening at the North Insurance office with James Otis, Solo. Davis, John Erving, Thos. Brattle, Capt. Vernon, Nat. Barber, Andrew Clark, and John White."

Club life as well as public festivities were mostly suspended after the battle of Lexington, except on special occasions like the visit of the French fleet.

The usual drives in the country were round Jamaica Pond or in Roxbury and Dorchester, sometimes "over the Neck round the little Square" (July 29, Aug. 10, 1774), and sometimes as far as Milton (April 6, 1769). Rowe often drove to Roxbury to see his old friend and relative Robert Gould, an invalid, till the latter's death early in 1772 (May 5, June 22, 1765). In the summer of 1771 he used to drive to Savin Hill, "a very agreeable rural spot," to a place which his friend Thomas Brattle had hired, where an agreeable company sometimes gathered for afternoon tea (May 16, June 3). The drive we may presume was often in a chaise; but sometimes Mrs. Rowe "took an airing in the chariot" (Sept. 2, 1766). The drives were to the south, as communication with the north was so circuitous. For instance, a party set out, Nov. 10, 1772, in Paddock's coach for Salem (Rowe's chaise accompanying it). "We went all round through Cambridge and dined at Martin's; we got to Salem about four of clock."

The suburbs of Boston were attractive in those as in later days. At Milton lived Thomas Hutchinson, in a house standing till 1872, which looked out on river and ocean in front and the Blue Hills in the rear, — a house then filled with sons and daughters. He loved that home on Unquity Hill, parted from it with deep regret, and sighed in exile to return to it. Rowe drove to Hutchinson's mansion to make calls, and sometimes on official business (June 16, Sept. 11, 1766; July 13, 1773). He had friendly relations with Daniel Vose, the merchant of the place, at whose house "at the Milton Bridge," still standing near the railway station, the Suffolk Resolves were passed; and dined there, May 6, 1769, in company with Dr. Catherwood, Joshua Winslow, Jr., and others. But the house in Milton which he sought the most was that of James Smith on Brush Hill, still standing, and for a long period the home of the late James M. Robbins. Smith, who died in 1769 at the age of eighty, was a wealthy sugar-refiner, and owned an estate of one hundred and seventy-one acres running to the Neponset River.[1] He had also a farm at Watertown, where he gave a distinguished dinner-party July 15, 1767. His second wife, Mrs. Elizabeth Campbell, born Murray, was of a Scotch family; and her maiden name is found in the middle names of her descendants, the late Mr. Robbins, and others who are still living in Milton. She became by a third marriage Rowe's kinswoman.[2] He records in a quaint way the courtship of herself and his brother-in-law Inman: July 22, 1771. "After dinner [at Rowe's] Mr. Inman introduced his design to Mrs. Smith." August 16. "Afternoon Mr. Inman and Mrs. Rowe paid a visit to Mrs. Smith over to Goldthwait's. Mr. Inman came home well pleased and agreed on his plan of matrimony." Rowe notes the publication of banns at King's Chapel, September 1, and the marriage "at the seat of Mr. Ezekiel Goldthwait," September 26, followed by a dinner at Inman's, where Rowe passed the evening and the night. Rowe was often at this Brush Hill house, once at least taking a sleigh-ride there (Jan. 30, 1765); and once Mrs. Rowe was badly bruised (Aug. 18, 1767) by her carriage being upset as she was driving there. It was Rowe's stopping-

[1] Pictures of the Hutchinson, Vose, and Smith houses are in Teele's "History of Milton."
[2] She and her second husband, James Smith, are buried at King's Chapel.

place as he was returning from fishing or business excursions (July 20, 1765; July 22, 1766). Under this roof often gathered gay dinner-companies, where were James Murray and wife; his daughters Anna, Betsey, and Dorothy[1] (the last afterwards the wife of Rev. John Forbes); old Madam Belcher, the Governor's widow, and Mrs. Belcher, widow of Andrew Belcher, who was both Madam's daughter and daughter-in-law; the Hoopers, Inmans, Vassalls, Amiels, Auchmutys, Goulds, Temples, Hallowells, Goldthwaits, Miss Blowers, Rev. Edward Winslow; and Milton neighbors, the Pratts and Clarks (March 28, July 19, 20, 1765; July 24, Oct. 23, 1766; Aug. 18, 1767; Feb. 7, 25, 1769). Rowe writes of the dinner, March 16, 1778, "We were very merry." These happy days at Brush Hill were then coming to a close, the greater number of the festive company sharing the fate of Loyalists and exiles. The Murray ladies succeeded in saving the estate itself from confiscation by remaining upon it and keeping very quiet during the war.[2]

There were then attractive houses at Cambridge. Rowe records festivities at several of them, — at Colonel Thomas Oliver's (Dec. 9, 1766; Feb. 22, 1768; Aug. 17, 1769), where were the Brattles, Temples, Vassalls, Byards, Phippses, Van Hornes, Edward Winslow, and Richard Lechmere; and at John and Henry Vassall's, where were similar companies (Feb. 16, 1765; Dec. 12, 1766; Feb. 17, 1768). His record for Feb. 20, 1768, was of a dinner at Ten Hills (Mr. Robert Temple's), where were "Mrs. Temple, Mrs. Elizth Hubbard, Miss Henrietta Temple and 4 daughters of Mr. Temple's, also Colo. James Otis, his son James Otis, Mr. Wm Bayard, Major Robt. Byard, Mr. Laviount, Mr. Dewar, Capt. Sheaffe of Charlestown, Colo. Saltonstall of Haverhill." A dinner at Colonel David Phipps's (July 7, 1768) has been noted elsewhere.

In no house in or about Boston were there more lavish entertainments than at Ralph Inman's in Cambridge, a house the site of which is just behind the present City Hall. No buildings then intervening to obstruct the view, it looked out on the Charles River and Boston beyond. Noble trees stood in

---

[1] She is buried at King's Chapel. Her portrait is in the possession of her grandson, John M. Forbes, of Milton.
[2] Teele's "History of Milton," pp. 173, 174, 421, 422.

the spacious grounds about it.[1] Rowe as a kinsman was often here for family and friendly gatherings, some of which have been elsewhere noted (Oct. 18, 1764; June 21, Aug. 2, Oct. 23, 1771; Aug. 25, 1773).

The entertainments at Inman's and at College rooms on Commencement Day surpass anything since known in that renowned home of culture and hospitality, except perhaps "the class spreads" given in recent years at the Hemenway Gymnasium and Beck Hall. Rowe makes these records: July 17, 1765. "Commencement Day. Went to Cambridge, Mrs. Rowe, Polly Hooper, and Sucky; dined at Edward Winslow's room, a very large company; went to Mr. Hooper's room, also to Col. Taylor's." Young Winslow was to die an exile in New Brunswick. The next day there was a dinner at Mr. Hooper's (probably Robert Hooper of the Class of 1765), "with a very large company"; and in the evening a dance at the Town House given by young Nathaniel Sparhawk, another of the Class of 1765, at whose request Rowe "officiated as master of the ceremony." Sparhawk and probably Hooper became Loyalists. A similar festivity is recorded July 16, 1766. Again, July 20, 1768: "I went to Cambridge, stopped at Mr. Inman's, dined with a very large company at Jos. Henshaw's, paid a visit to Tutor Hancock's, met the Rev⁴ Mr. Barnard of Marblehead, afterwards paid a visit to Mrs. Green's, where were a very large company, too many to enumerate." July 21. "A very hot day. I came to town this morning and returned to Cambridge; dined with Mr. David Greene, with a very large company, spent the evening there. We had a dance. I was master of the ceremonies; slept at Mr. Inman's." Greene of the Class of 1768 became a Loyalist. July 17, 1771: "I went to Cambridge and dined with Mr. Inman, Polly Jones, and Sally Inman; after dinner I went to Colo. Murray's room in the New Colledge,[2] where there was a large company, the Governour, Councill and too many to enumerate. I staid till six." Colonel John Murray and his son Daniel of the graduating class, also his son Samuel of the class of the following year, became Loyalists.

The fullest record of festivities at Cambridge is in July,

---

[1] Drake's "Historic Fields and Mansions of Middlesex," p. 187, gives a description and picture of the house.
[2] Hollis Hall.

1772. On the 15th Rowe dined at Samuel Murray's room, where were Colonel Murray the father, Colonel Saltonstall, Judge Sewall, Colonel Oliver, Samuel Quincy, Major Vassall, and many other guests whose names are given. Rowe adds: "After dinner we were visited by the Governour and Council, Admirall Montague and many other gentlemen too many to enumerate. I paid a visit to Mr. Jonathan Williams' son and also Dr. Whitworth's son, both which took their degree." The record of the next day is as follows: "I went early to Mr. Inman's, who made the genteelest entertainment I ever saw on account of his son George taking his degree yesterday. He had three hundred forty-seven gentlemen and ladies dined, two hundred and ten at one table, amongst the company the Governour and family, the Lieut.-Governour and family, the Admirall and family, and all the remainder gentlemen and ladies of character and reputation; the whole was conducted with much ease and pleasure, and all joyned in making each other happy; such an entertainment has not been made in New England before on any occasion." A ball at the Town House in Cambridge followed, where "all were very happy and cheerful," and Rowe slept at Inman's. George Inman, whose college life closed so merrily, left his home three years later to join the British army, and died at Grenada in the West Indies in 1789.

These annual festivities were approaching a suspension; and Rowe records, July 20, 1774, that "the distressed situation of the town and Province prevents Commencement Day being kept publick as usual." Inman's house became General Putnam's headquarters during the siege of Boston,—an event which is commemorated by an inscription on a stone slab placed on its site by the city of Cambridge. The building itself, removed twenty and more years ago, is now a double tenement house, recently bereft of its piazza, numbered 64 and 66 on Brookline Street in that city, and making the southeast corner of Brookline and Auburn streets.

Ralph Inman's estate escaped confiscation, and he returned to live and die upon it, and to bequeath it by a will proved in July, 1788. He has posterity other than the Linzees living in Boston, New York, and Philadelphia, descending from the daughters of his son George, who came with their mother from Grenada to Massachusetts soon after their father's death, and his sons Thomas, John, and Elbridge; and of Tristram Dalton at "Newberry Old Town," where Rowe dined, July 26, 1776, when returning from Portsmouth. Of Dalton's place he writes: "This seat of Mr. Dalton's is most delightfully situated, and has the most extensive prospect I ever saw, particularly of the River Merrimack and the sea beyond, Newberry Port and Hampton Beach."

One gets the impression from this Diary that in the days before the Revolution there was a country life in New England in large houses remote from Boston (not summer cottages only) more interesting and having greater social vitality than anything like it in those or similar localities in our time.

The public feasting in Boston at this time was beyond anything now seen in places of the same population. There were merchants' dinners, St. Patrick dinners, charitable society dinners, Masonic dinners, artillery election dinners, dinners on board vessels of war and commerce,[1] dinners at Faneuil Hall to celebrate the close of the school year, with clergymen and official or eminent persons as guests, dinners of the Proprietors of Long Wharf, dinners on Spectacle, Rainsford, and Noddle's islands, and at the Light House. There were dinners, often with dancing, to celebrate the King's accession to the throne, and the King's and Queen's birthdays, and to express the public joy at the repeal of the Stamp Act. Rowe was present at all these, often serving as chairman or toastmaster; and he describes with much zest the entertainments as "genteel." He seemed to enjoy more than any the Masonic dinners which came twice a year, in June and December; and he always gives the names of the brethren present. Dec. 27, 1764, he wrote: "I don't remember St. John, as long as I have belonged to the fraternity, has been celebrated with more decorum and more pleasure." The merchants' dinner at the Coffee House, Dec. 2, 1766, Rowe presiding, to Capt. John Gideon, commander of the warship "Jamaica," just before sailing, was a notable festivity. Here were all the principal merchants and citizens, including Hancock, Otis, Edmund Quincy, Cushing, the Boylstons, Amorys, and Hallowells. Rowe says: "And a very genteel entertainment it was." A committee, of which Rowe was a member, had been appointed the day before by the

[1] April 21, 1774, on board Rowe's own ship, the "Montagu."

town to express its thanks to Captain Gideon for his conduct while stationed at Boston.

Sometimes our ancestors feasted on a roasted ox, or "barbikue,"—"the ox being carried through the streets in triumph" the day before,—at the Turk's Head, on the Common, at Faneuil Hall, and Dennis Island (Sept. 28, 1764; Aug. 13, 1765; Aug. 1, 1766; Aug. 16, 1768; May 29, 30, 1770). These were not occasions for the masses only; but the leading people, ladies as well as gentlemen,—Hutchinsons, Olivers, Grays, Belchers, Sheaffes, Auchmutys, Swifts, and Goldthwaits,—took part.

The places for feasting when the company was very large were Faneuil Hall and Concert Hall,—the latter resort situated on the south corner of Court and Hanover streets, and standing till a modern period,[1]—but considerable parties were entertained at Mrs. Cordis's Coffee House; Colonel Joseph Ingersoll's Bunch of Grapes in King Street (Captain Marston was his successor there, 1775-1779); Bracket's, Gardner's, and King's Arms on the Neck; the Peacock, Greaton's (the Greyhound), Richards's, and Blany's in Roxbury; Kent's and John Champney's (the Turk's Head) in Dorchester; Coolidge's "at Watertown Bridge"; Weatherby's at Menotomy Pond, and places of refreshment at Fresh Pond and Spot Pond. These festivities included a pleasant suburban drive of ladies and gentlemen round Jamaica Pond (in winter in sleighs), a dinner and tea and a dance in the evening, joined in not by the young only, but also by middle-aged people of foremost rank in the town. Sometimes each paid his own score, but at other times one of the party was host and the rest guests. The French consul was the host at Marston's Feb. 27, 1779; and Colonel Dalrymple, Francis Waldo, and John Lane on other occasions at the Peacock (July 10, Aug. 20, Oct. 30, 1771).

Eighty gentlemen, "a high campaign," went, Aug. 11, 1767, to witness a launch at Weymouth. An excursion to a remoter point may be chronicled in this connection, Aug. 6, 1772: "This morning Mr. Hancock, Dr. Cooper, Mr. Brattle, Mr. Tuthill Hubbard, Mr. Saml. Calef, Mr. Winthrop of Cambridge, Mr. Nicho. Bowes and Capt. Hood went from Boston in the Providence packet to visit the eastern parts of this province and also on a party of pleasure. My servant Henry Smith and

[1] It was finally demolished in 1869.

Davis the barber's man went with them as attendants." The party returned August 22.

There were a succession of enjoyable inns on the highways leading from Boston southward to Plymouth and Taunton, and also to the east and west. Most sought by Rowe was Doty's,[1] in Stoughton, now Canton, just beyond the Blue Hills, standing till it was burned in December, 1888, its site now a race-course. Here met in 1774 the "County Congress," with Warren at the head of the Boston delegation, by which at an adjourned meeting held at the house of Daniel Vose in Milton were passed the famous Suffolk Resolves. Here during the siege lived Ezekiel Price, who drove often to Milton to learn the news and observe from the hill the movements of the British ships in the harbor. Rowe had occasion on fishing-excursions or journeys to Dighton on business (the affairs of Ebenezer Stetson, an insolvent debtor), to stop often at this tavern, and he managed whenever he could to pass the night there. Once when returning from Dighton, May 9, 1766, he wrote: "We supped and slept there, and I set it down as an extraordinary house of entertainment, and very good beds." Other country taverns which he frequented were Brackett's in Braintree, Deacon Cushing's in Hingham, Elisha Ford's in Marshfield, Spears's and Hall's in Pembroke, Howland's in Plymouth, Newcomb's in Sandwich, Stone's in Stoughton, Widow Noyes's in Sharon (then Stoughtonham, where one of the Edmund Quincys seemed to be an *habitué*), Howard's and Kingman's in Easton, McWhorter's in Taunton, Tapley's, Johnson's, and Norwood's in Lynn, Goodhue's in Salem, "a good tavern and good lodging" (Oct. 1, 1767), Treadwell's in Ipswich, Widow Ames's and Woodward's (both being the same)[2] and Gay's in Dedham, Mackintosh's in Needham, Pratt's at Needham Bridge, and Fisher's on Charles River in the upper part of that town, Bullard's in Natick (where Rowe dined July 8, 1765, "on fish which Mrs. Bullard dressed very well"), Mann's in Wrentham, and Bryant's in Sudbury. These

---

[1] An account of this tavern, with a picture, is given in Huntoon's "History of Canton," pp. 335–341.

[2] These taverns were in Dedham village. Mrs. Ames was the mother of Fisher Ames, and married Woodward for her second husband. At Woodward's, the "County Congress," which afterwards passed the Suffolk Resolves at Milton, met.

wayside inns, sometimes the resort of parties of gentlemen and ladies driving from Boston, appear attractive in Rowe's pages; but John Adams does not give so favorable an account of them.[1]

Fresh-water fishing was a great sport in those days, and Rowe was one of the jolliest and most expert fishermen. We read in John Adams's Diary (II. 238) a note, June 2, 1770, from Goldthwait to Adams, who was to start the next day for Portsmouth on a professional errand: "Do you call tomorrow and dine with us at Flax Pond near Salem. Rowe, Davis, Brattle, and half a dozen as clever fellows as ever were born, are to dine there under the shady trees by the pond upon fish and bacon and pease, &c.; and as to Madeira, nothing can come up to it. Do you call. We'll give you a genteel dinner and fix you off on your journey." Rowe took care to provide himself with all a fisherman's needs, as imported rods (June 11, 1765); sometimes "lost several fine hooks and snoods" (Sept. 10, 1768), once lost "the top of his rod line and hooks by a very large pickerell" (Sept. 17, 1764), and once left behind his "fishing rod and leather dram bottle" (Oct. 2, 1767). His companions on these excursions were often Samuel Calef or Henry Ayres, and sometimes his clerical friends. In the early part of the Diary he was fishing mostly in Flax Pond in Lynn, and in the latter part mostly in Charles River at Dedham and Needham, keeping a boat at Dedham, which he sent up the river, June 12, 1776, and stopping sometimes at Kendrick's or other taverns in the town or vicinity, but oftener at Richards's (probably Timothy Richards), who, though not a tavern-keeper, received him in a friendly way. Other fishing-resorts frequented by him were Menotomy Pond, with Wyndship's tavern near by; Fresh Pond; Spot Pond; Jamaica Pond; Ponkapoag Pond (Doty's tavern near by), and perhaps Houghton's in the vicinity (Aug. 2, 1766); Mossepong (or Massapoag) Pond (July 30, 1767) in Sharon; ponds or streams in Natick and Wrentham; "the Great Worster Pond"[2] in Shrewsbury, where he was entertained at "Mr Furnaces" and fished at "Worster Bridge" (May 12, 13, July 6, 1767); and a pond "at the upper end of Mallden" (July 2, 1767). To the south were sheets of water inviting

[1] Works, ii. 123, and elsewhere.
[2] Long Pond, or Lake Quinsigamond.

the fisherman,—in Hingham, Taunton, Duxbury, Pembroke, and Plymouth; and with all these Rowe was familiar.

Sometimes the luck was poor, but generally it was very good. Four or five dozen was an ordinary catch; but often the fishing-party brought back ten or even twenty dozen,—sometimes pickerel two feet long and weighing nearly four pounds (one caught June 29, 1770, weighing four and a quarter pounds); perch fifteen, sixteen, and eighteen inches long, and weighing three and a half pounds; and trout eighteen inches long. Sept. 22, 1764. "Went to Flax Pond, fished with Mr. Saml. Calef, had great sport; caught two pickerell, one was two foot long and weighed three pounds and three quarters, and about four dozen of large pond perch, one measured fourteen inches." At the same pond, July 29, 1766, twelve dozen perch were caught in two hours; and, June 19, 1772, very near one hundred weight were caught. July 13, 1765. "Early this morning went to Monotomy Pond with the Rev^d Mr. Auchmooty and Mr. Saml. Calef, had great sport; we caught above sixteen dozen of pond and sea perch, made a rough day of it, and came home in the evening." June 21, 1766, seven dozen perch were caught in the same pond. June 2, 1767. After a night at Mackintosh's tavern in Needham with Amiel, Calef, Jacobson, and Apthorp, Rowe makes the entry: "I rose very early this morning, routed up my companions, and set out for Bullard's Pond at Natick, where went a fishing; had extraordinary sport. We did not weigh the fish; I guess we caught about eighty weight. I caught about 25¾ lbs. weighed at Kendrick's. We came back and dined at Kendrick's, with old Madam Apthorp, Major Byard and lady, Mr. Amiel and wife, Mr. Inman and Mrs. Rowe, Mr. Spence and Miss Sally Sheaff, Capt. Jacobson, Mr. Saml. Calef, Mr. Thos. Apthorp, Mr. Robt. Apthorp, George Inman, and Jack Wheelwright. We were very merry." Returning from Taunton, where they had fished in Winnecunnet Pond, John Boylston and Rowe passed the night of July 31, 1767, at the Widow Noyes's in Sharon, after fishing in "Mossepong Pond." The entry of the next day is: "We went to Punkapong Pond and fished there; we caught 26 dozen of pond perch before ten of clock, which I told. We dined there; after dinner set out for Boston, and got in before dark." August 2. "John Boylston is a good companion, but very fretfull and uneasy in his make. I should be very glad to accompany him at any time on a party of fishing, especially when the fish bites fast." After a night at Doty's, Rowe, Jacobson, and Calef fished, Aug. 18, 1768, in the same pond; and the entry is: "Had great sport, caught upwards of twenty-seven dozen, and some large fish; dined at Doty's; after dinner set out for home, was caught in the rain, stopped at Mr. Clark's at Milton, drank tea there." Rowe and Admiral Montagu went a-fishing, June 9, 1773, in Wrentham Pond. Rowe "was a little unwell, and did not tarry; the admirall caught 173 perch." Rowe fished occasionally at "the Dedham causeway, beyond Dedham Island" (Sept. 30, 1766; June 13, 20, 1767; May 14, 1768). He records, June 7, 1766: "There's a trout brook empties itself into Charles River about a mile and half beyond Dedham Island causeway; dined under a large apple tree, and fished again."

Ladies were sometimes of the party, and passed the night at the tavern near by; but they do not appear to have joined in the sport. At Kendrick's on Charles River, July 27, 1765, Pitts, Bowdoin, Boutineau, Bourne, and Flucker were accompanied by their wives for the day, and Nicholas Boylston was of the party. At Doty's tavern in Stoughton the fishing-party was joined, Aug. 21, 1776, by "the two Mrs. Belchers, Miss Clark, Miss Dolly Murray, Mrs. Jones, Miss Blowers, Miss Amiel, Mr. Hutchinson, and Mr. Waller." At Flax Pond, June 29, 1770, the ladies of the Wendell, Goldthwait, Wells, Gerry, and Winslow families joined the party. June 8, 1773. Admiral Montagu's wife and other ladies were at Mann's tavern in Wrentham for the night, when Rowe and the Admiral were fishing there. Aug. 28, 1773. At Menotomy Pond were Montagu and his wife and daughter, Lady Frankland and Henry Cromwell, the ladies Lechmere, Simpson, Inman, Flucker, several military and naval officers, Commissioner Hulton, and Collector Harrison. "We were very jolly. The Admirall, Capt. Williams, and I had very poor luck, the fish very small."

Rowe, when visiting Plymouth for business or pleasure, did not fail to take advantage of ponds and brooks in that town and vicinity, — at Duxbury Mills, April 28, 1767, where five dozen trout were caught; at Pembroke, May 20, 1769, April 30, 1770, and May 5, 1773, each time catching fifty, fifty-eight, and sixty trout; at South Pond, Plymouth, Aug. 12, 1766, where he "caught a very large perch, measured 18 inches and weighed three pounds and half"; and May 31, 1771, when he had very good sport, afterwards dining at Mr. Richman's. "We were very merry; some young ladies came there a fishing and to pay a visit, particularly Miss Polly Brimhall of Plymouth and two daughters of Mr. Richman."

Fishing in this neighborhood gave Rowe a glimpse of Indian life, May 23, 1770: "We rose early [in Sandwich] and set out for Mashby, an Indian town. We took a guide, one Mr. Fowler. We reached Jos. Asher's, a native; we fished there, found it a wild place; we had good sport; from thence we went to Mr. Crocker's, the tavern; we dined there, and we were joyned by Capt. Solo. Davis, Mr. Calef, Mr. Brattle, and the Rev⁴ Mr. Hawly, the Indian minister, who I take to be a clever man; there were two young ladies, daughters of Mr. Crocker, Miss Bettsy and Miss Sally, very clever and genteel: from this we returned to Sandwich; we spent the evening and supped at Mr. Fessenden's, and were joyned by Melatiah Bourn and Doctor Smith of this place. We slept at Mr. Newcomb's; very good beds. We passed by the most beautiful pond, named Wakely. May 24. We rose early and set out for Plymouth; we slept at Ellis, and from thence got to the Monument, where we slept at Isaac Jeffery's, an Indian and a preacher to the Indians; his squaw had a neat wigwam. I slept an hour there. We dined there and were joyned by Silv' Barthlet. After dinner I went down to the river and caught ten trout, the largest I ever saw, severall of them eighteen inches in length; from thence we returned to Plymouth and spent the evening at Edw. Winslow's and all his family. I went to bed early and slept there." Another visit was made, May 6, 1772, to "the Indian wigwam of old Isaac at the Monument ponds," with a dozen very large trout as the result.

The hooking of turtles is sometimes recorded, — one at Fresh Pond, June 25, 1765, weighing thirty pounds. Except "trying for some smelts" once or twice (Oct. 5, 18, 1764), Rowe says nothing of salt-water fishing, although the harbor of Boston within the memory of living people has been good fishing-ground. He records, June 19, 1765, a strange apparition in our waters: "This morning our fishermen caught a large fish in the shape of a shark twenty foot long; his teeth were different from a shark's teeth." The next day's record is: "They cut up the fish, and filled two large hogsheads with his liver."

We have sports which were unknown to our fathers; but they had fine fishing-resorts within one or two hours' drive from Boston which we can only have by long journeys to the Rangeley Lakes and the Adirondacks.

In the period immediately preceding the Revolution, the port of Boston was a lively scene. War-vessels were leaving for or coming in from Halifax or the South or England, or going out on short cruises. The sailing and arrival of merchant vessels, several in a day, were town topics of keen interest. April 19, 1765. "Above thirty sail of vessells arrived from the Vineyard this afternoon." Rowe mentions the clearing of ships for Nova Scotia and New Brunswick, the West Indies, Lisbon, Oporto, Cadiz, Gibraltar, Alicante, Madeira, Surinam, Glasgow, Newcastle, Bristol, Plymouth, Whitby, London, or their arrival from those ports. Liverpool is mentioned once only in such a connection (May 24, 1768), that port not having then attained the prominence it has since held. Passages between English ports and Boston ranged from five to eight weeks; but Captain Bruce made the run from London (arriving Oct. 20, 1764) to Boston in twenty-six days, which Rowe mentions as "the shortest passage ever known."[1] Later he records a still shorter passage, April 20, 1769: "This afternoon Capt. Post arrived from Glasgow in a short passage of twenty-two days." Another short passage is noted May 8, 1767: "This day arrived Capt. Delano from London in 27 days passage."

Rowe notes the arrival, May 11, 1774, of a vessel from Scotland, with upwards of a hundred passengers,—the only instance of a body of immigrants mentioned in the Diary.

The town was not without commercial panics; and a serious one occurred in January, 1765. On the 16th Nathaniel Wheelwright "stopt payment and kept in his room. A great number of people will suffer by him. . . . The trade has been much alarmed." That evening at Mrs. Cordis's the conversation was on his affairs; and Mr. Inman went to the Assembly,

[1] There were shorter passages going eastward: Richard Clarke made one in twenty-one days (S. Curwen's Journal and Letters, p. 43); General Burgoyne made one "in less than twenty-four days" (Hutchinson's Diary and Letters, i. 567).

probably to start legislative action. On the 19th Rowe writes: "Very bad accounts. Mr. John Scollay shut up; Mr. John Dennie shut up, and Peter Bourne at the North End; am like to be a large sufferer by Scollay." January 20. "Was much out of order today, occasioned by the distress the town is in, occasioned principally by the failure of Mr. Wheelwright; was sent for this forenoon on my friend Jos. Scot's affairs, he seems greatly distressed. . . . Was sent for by Sheriff Greenleaf on John Scollay's affairs. Did not go to church, my mind too much disturbed." January 21. "Mr. Cudworth the sheriff came here on business, and Mr. Cary on affairs of Wm. Hoskings & Co., who shut up this morning, as did my friend Joseph Scot. A general consternation in town occasioned by these repeated bankruptcies. That the General Court which are now sitting determine to make an act for the relief of insolvent debtors,— which will be very seasonable." The General Court, in consequence of the application, passed the Act of March 9, 1765, which was approved by the Privy Council, though such an act had been disallowed eight years before. Scollay's and Wheelwright's estates were distributed under the new Act.[1]

Arbitration was usually resorted to by merchants for adjusting disputes which arose in the way of trade. Rowe and merchants of his standing often sat on such boards, which met usually at the Coffee House or Colonel Ingersoll's tavern. His records of such sessions are so frequent that it is not worth while to give the dates.

A minute of one lawsuit, March 19, 1765, may be given here: "Went to the Superiour Court in the forenoon and heard the learned debate before the judges in the case of John Banister and others. . . . Went in the evening and heard more argument in the case of John Banister and others; both Mr. Auchmooty and Mr. Otis behaved very well, and I was pleased with Mr. Dana in this argument."

Rowe's Diary discloses a great number of fires in Boston at this period. They started in many instances from foul chimneys and bakehouses. "'T was a terrible foul chimney," is a record he sometimes makes (Feb. 2, 1765). The citizens, it must be said to their credit, worked with energy and organization, and generally got the better of the fire before it spread

[1] Province Acts and Resolves, iv. 777-781, 793-795.

beyond the building where it started (Oct. 12, 1767). There were as early as 1768 as many as six fire-engines, and John Hancock gave another in 1772.[1] Rowe commends "the dexterity and clever behaviour of the South End Engine men" (Jan. 24, 1765). On April 2, 1768, when there were several alarms, "one poor man lost his life by falling off a ladder." The fire-wards were substantial citizens like Samuel Adams, Hancock, Captain Adino Paddock, Captain Thomas Dawes, John Scollay, and Rowe, who got excused from further service March 9, 1772. There was a Fire Club, already mentioned, which was composed of the most substantial citizens. Rowe went to the fires and fought them vigorously, coming home afterwards "much wet and tired," and going to bed (Jan. 18, 1765; June 15, 1766). His leathern bucket, marked, in large letters, "John Rowe, 1760," is still in the possession of his grand-niece, Mrs. Payson. On June 15, 1766, "after six a fire broke out at the North End, and consumed Dr. Clark's barn, and severall other houses took fire, but by the dexterity of the people we soon extinguished it." The jail was set on fire by two prisoners Jan. 29, 1767, but little damage was then done. Two years later it was burned down, putting the neighborhood in danger. Rowe wrote, Jan. 31, 1769: "The officers and army behaved extremely clever on this occasion, and ought to have the publick thanks of this town. I can truly say they were the means of saving it. I waited on Brigadier Pomroy and Colo. Kerr and thanked them for their behaviour." A fire (July 10, 1772) on the turf of the Common behind the powder-house alarmed the inhabitants. In the evening of May 17, 1775, "about eight of clock a terrible fire broke out in the barracks on Treat's Wharf occupied by the 65th regiment; it was occasioned by accident or rather from great carelessness; it destroyed 33 stores on Dock Square, mine was in great danger. I thought it so, and therefore removed great part of my effects from them; it continued till half past one with progress; the officers behaved very well; the cloathing of 4 companies belonging to the 47th regiment was burnt and some fire arms lost."

The most disastrous fire of the period was on Feb. 4, 1767, breaking out in "a baker's warehouse and spreading round

---

[1] Memorial History of Boston, iii. 151.

about the neighborhood, that it consumed more than twenty houses, among which were Mr. Jonathan Williams's dwelling-house, several houses of Mr. John Hancock, several belonging to Capt. Ball; it began at ten of clock and continued until three in the morning." Public and private charity was invoked in behalf of the sufferers, forty of whom were reduced to extreme poverty. The selectmen promptly sent a petition to the General Court asking for a grant of relief for the sufferers, and that body voted £400 to be paid to the selectmen for the purpose. The selectmen (Rowe being one) received a statement of losses, and distributed the fund March 6, 10, 12, 27. They addressed a letter to the churches, asking for contributions April 5. In Trinity Church, May 17, there was a collection for the sufferers by the late fire. "Mr. Walter behaved extremely clever on this occasion, and urged his congregation to their usual benevolence." The selectmen also distributed the fund which came from the churches (June 5, 12). A collection was taken, Aug. 7, 1768, in Trinity Church for sufferers by fire at Montreal. It is pleasant to note how the well-to-do people of Boston at that day were sympathetic, as they have been ever since, with others, near or remote, who were afflicted with misfortune.

Curiously enough, Rowe, who was keen in noting fires, makes no reference to that in Fish Street, Aug. 10, 1774, attended with loss of life, which is mentioned in Thomas Newell's Diary; but he notes, October 6 of the same year: "A large fire happened at Salem last night; Dr. Witaker's meeting house and eighteen houses were destroyed."

The lighting of the streets of London, the significance of which inspired a well-known passage of the third chapter of Macaulay's History, took place in the last year of Charles the Second's reign. Somewhat less than a century later this reform was introduced into Boston; and Rowe was one of its leaders, quite likely its originator. Thomas Newell's Diary mentions only the first lighting, and also his beginning (Jan. 8, 1774) to make the tops of the glass lamps; but Rowe gives in detail the progress of the enterprise, which occupied his attention for a year.[1] His first entry concerning it was, March 1,

[1] Rowe does not mention the loss of the first lamps sent from England by the wreck of a tea-ship off Cape Cod in December, 1773, — a fact stated in John Andrews's letters.

1773: "Afternoon I spent at Faneuil Hall with the committee about lighting the lamps; present myself, Henderson Inches, Wm. Phillips, Benj. Austin, and Mr. Appleton." Another meeting, May 18: "Attended the committee about fixing the lamps. We finished the north part of the town, No. 1, 2, 3, 4 and 5 divisions; present myself, Deacon Phillips, Deacon Storer, Thomas Gray, Mr. Appleton, Major Daws, to which were the gentlemen of the severall wards, Mr. Jonathan Brown, Mr. John Leach, Mr. Paul Revere, Mr. Edward Procter, Mr. Thos. Hitchman." May 24. "This day I went with the committee about the lamps to view the wards No. 6, 7, and 8, which we finished." The same names of persons present recur, with the addition of John and Thomas Amory, Deacon Church and Major Paddock, and others. Records of various meetings are given, namely: May 4, 10, 13, Sept. 7, 24, 27, 1773, and Jan. 8, Feb. 1, 3, March 21, 22, 24, 1774. Rowe "attended [Jan. 19, 1774] the carpenter and blacksmith in marking out the places the lamps are to be fixt." The next day, he and others — the selectmen and the committee — "consulted on the method of lighting them, and had a long conference with Mr. Smith for that purpose." The end was reached March 2; and Rowe's entry the next day is, "Last evening the lamps were lighted for the first time; they burnt tolerably well." The final report of the committee was accepted in town-meeting March 30.

Pope's Day, November 5, with its rival North End and South End processions, and their contest or "battle," sometimes at Mill Bridge on Hanover Street, is described by Rowe. In 1764 the sheriff, justices, and militia undertook to destroy the figures, but the populace was too much for them. Several thousand people were in attendance, and there was a fatal injury. This "foolish custom," as Rowe calls it, became in later years, as in 1769, 1773, and 1774, less of an affair, and then died out altogether.

The lottery still existed in this Puritan community, legalized for public objects. Rowe bought, March 19, 1767, seven tickets of John Ruddock, and sold one, kept two for himself, and gave the rest to Mrs. Rowe and the Inmans.

The fashion of duelling still lingered, Feb. 23, 1765: "Colo. Bourn of M'head and Jerahmiel Bowers challenged each other with sword and pistoll yesterday about the excise." Oct. 10,

1773. "There was a duel fought between Capt. Maltby of the Glasgow man of war and Lieut. Finney of the Marines on Noddle's Island yesterday. Lieut. Finney was wounded in the breast, and its thought mortally."

Rowe gives incidents of crimes and punishments, Sept. 11, 1764: "The regiment appeared in the Common this afternoon. One of the soldiers behaved saucily to his captain, upon which they called a court martial and ordered him to ride the wooden horse; but the mob got foul of the wooden horse and broke it, so that the fellow escaped." Oct. 4, 1764. "Went after dinner upon Boston Neck and saw John and Ann Richardson set on the gallows for cruelly and wilfully endeavoring to starve their child [or children]; the man behaved in the most audacious manner, so that the mob pelted him, which was what he deserved." March 21, 1765. "This day a woman was tryed for murther of her bastard child, and it appearing to the court she was married, she was acquitted." Jan. 11, 1770. "This day a villain was pilloried for forcing a girl of ten years age. The populace pelted him severely, but not so much as his crime deserved." March 28, 1771. "This day the French boy and a charcoal fellow stood in the pillory. The French boy was to have been whipt, but the populace hindred the sheriff doing his duty." Oct. 21, 1773. "Levi Ames was hanged this afternoon, many thousand spectators attended the execution."[1] Ames's offence was burglary; and other burglaries where Rowe himself was the victim are noted in the Diary (July 3, 1767; April 5, 1773; March 7, 1779).

Boston does not seem to have been the orderly and well-governed town which our fathers sometimes proclaimed it to be. There was no constabulary force which amounted to anything when such a force was required. The mobs of Pope's Day, as already seen, had their own way, defying even the militia. The populace arrested at pleasure the infliction of public punishments judicially ordered, and sometimes superadded discretionary pelting of their own (Sept. 11, Oct. 4, 1764; Jan. 11, 1770; March 28, 1771). When the political troubles came, they sacked and destroyed the houses of unpopular citizens and magistrates. They stripped the offender naked, covered him with tar, decked him with feathers, and transported him in this plight, without hindrance, through the main thoroughfares

[1] Memorial History of Boston, ii. 486.

as a spectacle for a jeering multitude (Oct. 28, 1769; May 18, 1770; March 9, 1775). One cannot help asking where at such times were the selectmen, the twelve constables, the militia, Hancock and his Cadets, and the principal citizens who were so effective when fires were to be extinguished or patriotic enterprises to be executed. On the whole, Boston is now a safer place to live in for one who asserts the right to differ with his neighbors than it was in those good old days.

There were at this time in Boston nearly one thousand negro slaves,[1] of whom Rowe owned two or three. He mentions, Nov. 22, 1766: "Last night I sent my negro Cato to Bridewell for a very bad fault," which is not described; and Jan. 20, 1768, he disposes of Cato by sending him to Jamaica. Another or the same Cato appears on the scene Jan. 4, 1769: "When I came home I found Cato has got a soldier's sword which belonged to Capt. Fordyce's company of the 14th Grenadiers, his name James Fairchild." Nov. 25, 1769. "I sent Cato on board the Rose man of war this morning." Sept. 23, 25, 1772. "My negro Marcellus was brought home last evening much hurt." "I got all the fellows taken up that abused Marcellus and tryed them before Justice Quincy; the Justice ordered them to goal." Boston people, as appears by an entry Feb. 28, 1765, had interests in West India plantations: "This afternoon Mr. Henry Vassall and wife executed the deeds for the farm of negroes at Antigua."

The mere mention of some casualties or personal incidents may be of interest. March 24, 1765, there was the highest tide Rowe "had known since he had been in New England, accompanied with the greatest storm, and almost incredible damage," driving vessels from their anchors and dismasting and sinking them, with great injury to wharves, — to Rowe's in particular of two thousand pounds; but he adds, with resignation, "As it's the Providence of God, I am content about it." High tides, with more or less injury, occurred Dec. 26, 1764, and Oct. 20, 1770. Rowe records a providential escape Sept. 24, 1767: "The sun past the equinox about 12 of clock last night. We had a very severe storm; it blew as hard as I ever heard it, accompanied with thunder, lightning, and very heavy rain.

[1] Memorial History of Boston, ii. 439, 485.

21, 22, 28; Dec. 16, 1772; July 29, Aug. 6, 1773); the letting of Deer Island and Boston Neck by the town (April 15, 1766); the proposed sale of the town house (Feb. 6, 9, 1767); forty-eight applications for license to sell liquors (Aug. 6, 1766), and Rowe's sale of his still-house (May 8, 1769); women of a nameless class routed by a mob at Oliver's dock (July 24, 1771); a new pier head for Long Wharf (April 7, 1768); the paving of the road by the fortifications (May 25, 26, 1767); the laying out of a new street in Paddy's Alley (April 8, 13, 16, 1767); Thomas Hancock's gift for a lunatic asylum, and the assignment of a site for it on the Common (Sept. 19, 1764; March 23, 25, 1765); Dr. Cooper's election as President of Harvard College (Feb. 7, 1774), and his refusal three days later to accept the choice, "to the great joy and satisfaction of his parishioners"; a visit of the selectmen (March 10, 1768) to "Mary Phillips, who was born deaf and dumb and has remained so ever since, and is now upwards of eighty years of age"; the Superior Court "making a splendid appearance" in the new Court House (March 14, 1769); the payment of fees to lawyers, a guinea each to John Adams at Taunton (Aug. 19, 1766) and to James Otis in Boston (Nov. 20, 1766).

Extracts from John Rowe's Diary,
1764–1779.

1764. *Sept.* 29. — The Black Act takes place this day. Mr. Cockle [James Cockle, the Collector] suspended from his office yesterday at Salem, which the people at that place rejoiced at by firing guns, making bonfires, entertainments, &c.; and the Surveyor-General much applauded by the merchants in the town of Boston for his good and spirited behaviour.

October 2. — Went to the Collector's and Surveyor-Generall's about the Molasses Act, who agreed the Advocate-General should determine the method of gauging molasses, whether should be Winchester measure or wine measure.

Dec. 3. — Spent the evening with the committee of merchants and others about the loaf sugar; present Jos. Winslow, Esq., Mr. Thos. Gray, Mr. Edwd Paine, Mr. Richard Clark, Ezekiel Goldthwait, Mr. James Warden, Mr. Thos. Ivers, Capt. Solomon Davis, Mr. John Dennie, Mr. Melatiah Bourne; voted that Mr. Ivers bring an action at this Court against Mr. Collector for taking the duty of five shilling ster^g per hundred on loaf sugar cleared out at his office.

1765. *Jan.* 11. — Went after dinner to the Court and heard the tryal between Mr. Ivers and Mr. Hale [Roger Hale, the Collector] relative to the duties on loaf sugar; very warm debates on both sides, but the jury found for the plaintiff Mr. Ivers, which was generally thought a good verdict.

Feb. 12. — [Meeting of merchants with a committee of the General Court (names being given) on the Excise Act, with choice of Samuel Wells, Robert Hooper, and Justice Story as managers.]

Feb. 13. — [Petitioners on account of the Excise heard on the floor of the House.]

May 30. — Went in the evening at Blodget's with a number of the General Court, where they were shoeing colts, — that is, the new members that are chosen treat the Council and House of Representatives.

July 24. — Mr. Gerry came to town and brought an account of the Niger man of war taking three schooners out of the harbor of St. Johns, one belonging to his father and two to Epps Sergeant.

Aug. 11. — Capt. Harlow arrived from Bristol and brought the good news that Mr. Pitt was again in the ministry. [Pitt, though consulted, did not then enter the ministry.]

Aug. 14. — A great number of people assembled at Deacon Elliot's Corner to see the Stamp officer hung in effigy, with a libel on his breast, on Deacon Elliot's tree, and along side him a boot stuffed with representation which represented the Devill coming out of Bute; this stamp officer hung up all day; at night they cut him down, layd him out and carried in triumph amidst the acclamations of many thousands who were gathered together on that occasion. They proceeded from the So. End down the main street through the Town House and round by Oliver's dock, they pull'd down a new building which some people thought was building for a Stamp Office and did some mischief to Mr. Andrew Oliver's house (which I think they were much to blame).

Aug. 16. — Heard that Mr. Andrew Oliver had resigned his commission in form, on which there was great rejoicing the last evening in Boston.

[Vol. II. of the Diary, pp. 185–322, from Aug. 17, 1765, to April 10, 1766, is missing.]

1766. *April* 13. — Sunday. When I came home [from church] I heard of an Express being brought to town giving an account of the repeal of the Stamp Act, which I examined into and found the greatest probability of its being true, and pass'd by the House of Commons on Feby the 8th last by a great majority, which appeared by a letter of that date from Messrs. Day and Son to Mr. Maxwell, their correspondent in Petaxion [Patapsco or Patuxent] River, Maryland.

April 14. — The Selectmen met this forenoon to consider and fix on a day for rejoycing.

April 15. — Capt. Calef arrived from London this afternoon; he left the Downs the 20th Feby. He brought good news about our American affairs, but no certainty of the repeal of the Stamp Act.

April 18. — Capt. McClean arrived from Ireland, and confirms the account of the Stamp Act being repealed.

April 21. — A town meeting this forenoon to agree on a method of rejoicing and illuminations.

May 16. — Capt. Shuball Coffin arrived from London about 11 of clock and brought the glorious news of the total repeal of the Stamp Act, which was signed by his Majesty King George the 3^d of ever glorious memory, which God long preserve and his illustrious house.

May 19. — This day is the joyfull day indeed for all America, and all the people are to rejoyce this day for the joyfull news brought by these vessells from London, that the Stamp Act is repealed. Dined at Colo. Ingersoll's with twenty-eight gentlemen [names given]. We drank fifteen toasts; and very loyal they were, and suited to the occasion. In the evening there was very grand illuminations all over the town; in the Common there was an obelisk very beautifully decorated, and very grand fireworks were displayed. Mr. Hancock behaved very well on this occasion, and treated every person with cheerfulness. I contributed as much to the general joy as any person; the whole was much admired, and the day crowned with glory and honour.

May 23. — [At Colonel Murray's in Rutland.] In the evening they had great rejoycings at Rutland; they behaved very well, had a large bonfire and many sky rocketts which I put them in a way to fire; there was a genteel entertainment at the tavern; afterwards we returned to Colo. Murray's, where there was a grand supper and entertainment prepared and many loyal healths drank.

May 28. — Election day. Mr. Otis was chosen Speaker of the House, but negatived by the Governour. Mr. Saml. Adams, who has a great zeal for liberty, was chosen Clark of the House by one vote.

May 29. — Mr. Thomas Cushing was chosen Speaker in the room of Mr. Otis, who the Governour approved off. This day the Governour negatived six counsillors, viz.: Colo. Otis, Colo. Sparhawk, Colo. Gerrish of Newberry, Colo. Bowers of Swanzey, Mr. Dexter of Dedham, and Mr. Saunders of Gloster: this occasions great murmurings in some and rejoycings in others. Spent part of the afternoon with the House of Representatives, in shoeing colts.

June 2. — Artillery election. . . . Dined by invitation with the Govr and Council at Faneuil Hall; spent part of the afternoon at Mr. John Hancock's.

June 4. — The King's birthday and a great holliday.

June 10. — General Ruggles and Mr. Otis had some disputes and hard language this day on the floor of the Town House.

Sept. 24. — The Custom House attempted to seize some wine out of Malcom's cellar, but were hindered from it by about two hundred people making their appearance in the street. The Governour and Council met on this affair of the seizure, but they could make nothing of it.

Sept. 25. — The Governour and Council met again on this affair, and examined many evidences, but could make nothing of it.[1]

Nov. 25. — Spent the afternoon with the committee of the General Court, Mr. Speaker, Mr. Otis, Mr. Stephen Hall, Mr. Adams, Mr. Hancock, Mr. Dexter. A number of merchants were there; am in hopes we shall get redress in our trade.

Dec. 2. — [An account of a dinner given at the Coffee House by the merchants to Captain Gideon of the man of war the "Jamaica," at which Rowe presided. All the leading merchants were there, with Hancock, Cushing, and Otis, and twenty loyal toasts drunk, including those to the King and Queen and royal family, and the friends of America, — Chatham, Conway, Barré, and others.]

1767. *March* 13. — The General Court chose commissioners to treat with the Government of New York about the line between them and us, the Lieut.-Governour, Colonel Brattle, and Mr. Sheaff of Charlestown.

March 18. — Wednesday. This is anniversary day when the Parliament of Great Britain repealed the Stamp Act [celebrated by "a very genteel dinner" at Colonel Ingersoll's tavern, attended by the principal citizens, who are named, with Rowe as toastmaster]. At four of clock in the afternoon I was obliged to attend at Faneuil Hall, where there met a great concourse of people to drink the King's health, &c., and vote of the town and the same toasts were drank as above. The hall was illuminated, also Liberty Tree, and sundry other gentlemen's houses. I never saw more joy than on this occasion.

May 28. — The Governour negatived five counsillors this morning, the Honble. James Otis, Joseph Gerrish, Esq., Thos. Saunders, Esq., Jerahmiel Bowers, Esq., and Saml. Dexter, Esq.

Aug. 14. — This day the colours were displayed on the Tree of Liberty, and about sixty people, Sons of Liberty, met at one of clock and drank the King's health.

Aug. 22. — Mr. Hancock's Union flagg was hoisted for the first time.

Nov. 20. — Attended the trial of thieves, and the town meeting which was conducted with great propriety and moderation. Capt. Blake arrived this afternoon, which saved the freighters above three hundred pounds lawful money, this being the time fixed to pay the dutys on glass, painters' colours, &c., an imposition on America in my opinion as dangerous as the Stamp Act.

[1] Rowe was placed by the town, Oct. 8, 1766, on a committee with Otis, Hancock, Adams, and others to obtain copies of these depositions, which it had been proposed to have transmitted to the home government.

Dec. 4. — Spent the afternoon with the committee for giving instructions to the representatives, Rich⁴ Dana, Esq., Mr. Edw⁴ Payne, Dr. Church, Mr. Henderson Inches and Ezek¹ Price.

1768. *Feb.* 11. — Spent the evening at the Coffee House, and a disagreeable evening it was. The topick of the discourse was about the seizure made by Capt. Folger, and the reseizure of it afterwards by Capt. Hallowell. Mr. Mollineaux, in his representation and talk, used the Surveyor-General, Mr. Temple, most cruelly and barbarously; he abused the character of said gentleman most shamefully, and said that if Mr. Folger made any seizures or held this, that it would not be of any benefit to him, upon which one of the company asked Mr. Mollineaux who then would receive the benefit of Mr. Folger's part as informer, &c., and he reply'd "why are you at a loss, why Mr. Temple the Surveyor-General," and further said that there was an agreement between the Surveyor-General and Mr. Folger, intimating that the Surveyor-General gave Folger his place with a view to get money by it, and swore he believed it, — he Mr. Mollineaux was asked by Mr. John Erving "surely you can't believe the Surveyor-General guilty of so base a design, and you have behaved very ill in making the company think so," his reply was severall times "I do believe it," upon which Mr. Erving and Mollineaux had some smart speeches with each other; some of the company were very uneasy at these doings, and mentioned the commission that Folger had received from the Surveyor-General to be doubtfull and not authentick enough to make seizures. Upon which Mr. Otis said the commission he thought was very good, but that there was one expression in it that some people hesitated about, and repeated the sentence in the commission, which runs thus, "and in my behalf to seize for his Majesty's use," — upon repeating of this sentence Mr. Mollineaux [said] "now gentlemen, you see that I am right in what I have said," and seemed to lay great stress upon these words ("and in my behalf"), signifying that whatever seizures were made by Folger, he the said Folger was not to have the profit arising from such seizures but the Surveyor-General, and that the Surveyor-General gave him his commission on these terms. I mentioned in the course of this talk that I had many times been in Mr. Mollineaux's company, but never heard him guilty of so great an indiscretion before. Present Solo. Davis, John Erving, George Bethune, James Otis, Wm. Mollineaux, Thos. Gray, James Warden, myself.

12 *Febr'y.* — Fryday. Dined at home with the Rev⁴ Mr. Walter, Mr. Tristram Dalton of Newberry, Mr. Rich⁴ Letchmere, Mrs. Rowe, and Sucky and Sally Inman present. Spent the evening at Mrs. Cordis with Treas' Gray, Thos. Gray, Ezek¹ Goldthwait, Melatiah Bourn, Solomon Davis, Mr. Tristram Dalton, John Erving, Edward Payne, James Otis, and James Perkins. Mr. Mollineaux was there and renewed his discourse as on the last evening, but soon went away.

March 1. — Spent the evening at the Merchants' Meeting. Wm. Phillips, Esq., was chose moderator; there were 98 merchants present. They voted that it is the opinion of this company that every legal measure for freeing the country from the present embarrassments should be adopted, and among [them] the stopping the importation of goods from Great Britain under certain limitations, then chose a committee of nine to fix on and report to this company on adjournment the best measures for carrying into execution the foregoing vote. The following gentlemen were chosen: Myself, Wm. Phillips, Esq., John Hancock, Esq., Arnold Wells, Esq., Mr. Edward Payne, Mr. Thomas Boylston, John Erving, Jun., Esq., Melatiah Bourne, Esq., Mr. Henderson Inches; it was also voted that John Hancock, Esq., be desired to procure a coppy of the commissions of the Commissioners of the Customs and produce the same at the next meeting; then the meeting was adjourned untill Fryday evening.

March 3. — Spent the forenoon with the committee of merchants. Spent the afternoon and part of the evening with the committee of merchants, and part of the evening with the Charitable Society at Colo. Ingersoll's.

Mar. 4. — This day the Gov' prorogued the Assembly to the 13 April. Spent the day with the same committee of merchants, and in the evening we reported to them as follows:

The committee of merchants appointed at their [meeting] March 1st, 1768, having duly considered what they had in charge, do report the following resolutions, viz.:

In consideration of the great scarcity of money which has for several years been so sensibly felt among us, and now must be rendered much greater not only by the immense sums absorbed in the collection of the dutys lately imposed, but by the great checks given thereby to branches of trades which yielded us the most of our money and means of remittance, —

In consideration also of the great debt now standing against us which, if we go on increasing by the excessive imports we have been accustomed to while our sources of remittance are daily drying up, must terminate not only in our own and our country's ruin, but that of many of our creditors on the other side of the water, —

In consideration further of the danger from some late measures of our losing many inestimable blessings and advantages of the British Constitution, which Constitution we have ever rever'd as the basis and security of all we enjoy in this life, therefore

Voted

1st That we will not for one year send for any European commoddity excepting salt, coals, fishing lines, fish hooks, hemp, duck, bar lead, shot, wool cards, and card wire, and that the trading towns in the province and other provinces in New England together with those in New York, New Jersey and Pennsilvania be invited to accede hereto.

2nd That we will encourage the produce and manufactures of these colonies by the use of them in preference to all other manufactures.

3rd That in the purchase of such articles as we shall stand in need of, we will give a constant preference to such persons as shall subscribe to these resolutions.

4th That we will in our separate capacitys inform our several correspondents of the reasons and point out to them the necessity of witholding our usual orders for their manufactures [in order that] the said impediment may be removed and trade and commerce may again flourish.

5th That these votes or resolutions be obligatory or binding on us from and after the time that these, or others singular or tending to the same salutary purpose, be adopted by most of the trading towns in this and the neighbouring colonies.

6th That a committee be appointed to correspond with merchants in the before mentioned towns and provinces and forward to them the foregoing votes, and that s'd committee be impowered to call a meeting of the merchants when they think necessary.

March 9 & 11. — [Meetings of the merchants' committee, the one on the 11th lasting the whole day.]

March 18. — [Anniversary of repeal of the Stamp Act celebrated with dinner and toasts at Colonel Ingersoll's.] After these the company were very cheerfull and gay, and broke up about eight of clock. A considerable mob of young fellows and negroes got together this evening and made great noise and hallooing; about eight hundred appeared in King Street and at Liberty Tree, and went to the North to John Williams, the Inspector-General, but did him no damage, which the greatest part of the gentlemen in town were very glad of. There were two effigies on Liberty Tree this morning marked C. P. and J. W., but were taken down again by Wm. Speakman, Thos. Crafts, and John Avery, Junior.

March 21. — I spent the forenoon at the Court House to hear the tryal between Capt. Folger and Capt. Hallowell about the seizure of tea, and after the whole morning debates it was adjourned untill next Saturday morning. Spent part of the afternoon with the town's committee to draw a letter of thanks to the Farmer [John Dickinson] for his ingenious letters; present Dr. Church, Dr. Warren, Mr. Saml. Adams, and myself.

March 22. — Attended the town meeting all the day, in which many debates about Mr. Adams, whose friends were so warm in his favor that the gentlemen could not get a reconsideration of the vote passed on Monday last [which related to Adams's accounts as collector of taxes].

May 2. — Met the merchants at the Town House in the Representatives' room; agreed to the resolutions of the City of New York not to write for any goods after the first of June, nor import any after the first day of October untill the Act imposing dutys on glass, paper, &c., be repealed.

May 18. — The Romney man of war, Capt. Cornell [Corner] arrived yesterday in Nantasket, and this day in Kingroad.

June 10. — Yesterday the Selectmen viewed the ground for a gun house and the north battery. A considerable mob tonight occasioned by a seizure belonging to Mr. John Hancock; some damage to Mr. Harrison the Collector, and his boat burnt.

June 13. — The Selectmen waited on the Gov? and Council about Capt. Corner's pressing a man out of a coaster, and the affairs of the town.

June 14. — The people assembled under Liberty Tree, from thence removed to Faneuil Hall; then it was proposed to have a regular town meeting called, which was accordingly done. Afternoon the town met at Faneuil Hall; the people were so many that Mr. Otis the moderator proposed adjourning to Dr. Sewall's meeting, which was accordingly voted, and they met there. A committee of twenty-one gentlemen were chose to wait upon Govr Bernard with a humble petition, which petition to him is on file, and I think a very smart petition. The whole twenty-one met at Mr. John Hancock's, and proceeded in form to Roxbury to wait on Govr Bernard. Mr. Otis, being chairman, introduced the petition with a genteel speech. The Govr received us very cordially, spoke very sensibly to some parts of the speech and petition, and promised an answer in the morning. The committee returned to Mr. Hancock's in order as follows: —

Mr. Otis,	Mr. Hancock first,
Mr. Royal Tyler,	Mr. Thos. Cushing,
Myself,	Mr. Samuel Adams,
Mr. Joshua Henshaw,	Col. Joseph Jackson,
John Ruddock, Esq.,	
Mr. Henderson Inches,	Mr. Saml. Pemberton,
Mr. Edward Payne,	Mr. Melatiah Bourn,
Mr. Richard Dana,	Mr. Benjn Kent,
Mr. Samuel Quincy,	Mr. Josiah Quincy, Junr.,
Dr. Church,	Dr. Warren,

Dr. Young and Capt Daniel Malcom, all in carriages.

June 15. — The man of war the Romney unmoored. The town met again at Dr. Sewall's meeting.

June 16. — Spent the afternoon with the town's committee to draw instructions to the representatives on the present difficultys that attend the trade of this town, myself, Dr. Warren, Dr. Church, Mr. John Adams, Mr. Dana, and Mr. Henderson Inches. The Selectmen were ordered to attend the Govr and Council to hear the report of their committee and their consultations with Capt. Corner of his Majesty's ship the Romney.

June 17. — Spent the forenoon with the same committee as yesterday. Town meeting in the afternoon.

June 18 *and July* 3. — [Arrival of his Majesty's sloop, the Beaver.]

June 30. — This day the General Court behaved very steadily and according to the approbation of most good people who have any regard for their country and posterity, [voting] that they would not rescind their former resolutions which the Earl of Hillsborough took offence at, vide newspapers. Number of votes in the House, 109: 17 yeas, 92 nays. For my own satisfaction I record the seventeen yeas that were so mean spirited to vote away their blessings as Englishmen, namely, their rights, liberty and propertys.

July 8. — The Senegall man of war, Capt. Cookson, arrived here this day.

July 16. — Rose early [at Flax Pond, Lynn] and went fishing; dined at Mrs. Graves'; came home, and Mrs. R. told me of the Sons of Liberty visiting Mr. Williams the evening before, and that he engaged to meet them on the Change this day, which he did, and great numbers, she says, were present; he asked them what questions they had to ask him that he might answer them, but no person made him any reply. [This relates to John Williams, Inspector-General of the Customs.]

July 18. — Spent the afternoon with the committee of merchants at the Coffee House. Present myself, John Hancock, Edward Payne, Henderson Inches, Melatiah Bourn, and Thomas Boylston.

July 29. — This forenoon the Governour and Council met on affairs of consequence, its supposed relative to the introduction of troops, which has greatly alarmed the inhabitants.

Aug. 1. — Spent the afternoon at the general merchants' meeting at Faneuil Hall, at which place there were present sixty-two, sixty of which signed an agreement I have on file not to import any goods. Spent the evening at Mr. Barber's insurance office; and the silver bowl was this evening for the first time introduced, No. 45 weighs 45 ounces, holds 45 gills. [Present Hancock, Otis, Adams, and others.]

Aug. 2. — The committee of merchants met and got further subscriptions. [The Diary records many of these meetings.]

Aug. 8. — The merchants met at Faneuil Hall, present about 100.

Aug. 15. — Dined at Greaton's with a number of gentlemen [Hancock, Otis, Samuel Adams, Warren, Church, Josiah Quincy, Paul Revere, Scollay, Brimmer, and others], about one hundred, who were very jovial and pleasant, and in the forenoon a great number of people were at Liberty

Hall, where there was a variety of good musick exhibited, and great joy appeared in every countenance, being the anniversary day of the Sons of Liberty.

Sept. 9. — The Governour told me in conversation yesterday morning that he had staved off the introducing troops as long as he could, but could do it no longer.

Sept. 20. — Afternoon I attended the Selectmen and waited on the Council to consult about barracks for the troops that are expected.

Sept. 23. — King's coronation day. The convention met at Faneuil Hall this day.

Sept. 28. — This forenoon came to anchor in Nantasket Road six sail of men of war, supposed to have the 14th Regmt. and 29th Regiments on board.

Sept. 29. — Arrived three more of his Majesty's ships of war from Halifax, so that are now in our harbour [names of eleven vessels and their commanders given].

Oct. 1. — This day the troops came ashore, the 14th and 29th Regiments and two companies of the 59th, with a company of artillery; they marched into the Common. Colo. Dalrymple summoned the Selectmen; they all met and did not think themselves obliged to take cognizance for their being quartered in town, so that the 29th pitched their tents in the Common, the 14th got into Faneuil Hall, and part of the 59th at Rob' Gordon's stores.

Oct. 2. — Sunday. I went to the Coffee House to pay a visit to Mr. Edington, and was most smartly accosted by Capt. Dundass [commander of one of the fleet just arrived] in the following words: "Hah, John, are you there? Dammy, I expected to have heard of your being hanged before now, for damn you, you deserve it" — upon which I made reply, "Surely, Capt. Dundass, you're joking." Upon which he answered, "No, damn him if he was, for you are a damn incendiary, and I shall see you hanged in your shoes," and repeated the same; upon which I says to him, "Then you are in earnest, are you. I was in hopes you were joking." "No," he repeated, "damn you, I am in earnest. I tell you, you are an incendiary, and I hope to see you hanged yet in your shoes." I took notice who were present, as it was spoke about twelve of clock at noon. Mr. Forrest, Mr. Philip Dumaresqu, Mr. George Brinly, and several officers of the army who I did not know in the Coffee Room and entry way. I thought it prudent not to take any notice of it just then, but came home to dinner.

Oct. 10. — Last night some villains cut the frame of the Guard House so as to render it useless. Some people make light of this affair, but I think the scoundrels who did it ought to be severely punished, and I wish they may be found out.

Oct. 15. — Generall Gage arrived from New York at Major Byard's at Roxbury. The regiments were under arms and made a good appearance. The Generall with his attendants came into town about 4 P. M. The artillery saluted with 17 guns; they past and marched along the front of both regiments, and Capt. Willson's two companies who were formed in the center.

Oct. 16. — Sunday. This morning I waited on Colo. Robertson, who came with General Gage; he received me very politely. I had a full hour's discourse with him about the troops. I find him to be a gentleman of great abilitys and very cool and dispassionate. I took a walk [after afternoon service] and met General Gage and Colo. Dalrymple. General Gage engaged me to wait on him to-morrow morning.

Oct. 17. — I paid Genl. Gage a visit on business, who received me very kindly.

Oct. 22. — Waited on Colo. Maitland, Adjutant-Generall, to provide a division for the King's gunpowder in the magazine; also attended Genl. Gage and Colo. Robertson.

Oct. 23. — Sunday. The Honble. John Temple Esq.'s child was christened this forenoon at our church. The sponsors were Genl. Gage, Robert Temple, Esq. and his lady, by the name of Greenville.

Oct. 24. — Dined at home with Generall Gage, Colo. Robinson, Colo. Dalrymple, Capt. Smith of the Mermaid, Colo. Maitland, Colo. Kerr, Capt. Kimball, Major Gambell, Capt. Sheriff, Capt. Matrin, the Genl.'s Secretary, Mr. Inman, Mrs. Rowe, and Sucky.

Oct. 25. — The Romney sailed for Halifax. I waited on Colo. Robertson this morning. The regiments mustered this day in the Common and made a fine appearance. Colo. Dalrymple paid me a visit this evening. King's coronation day.

Oct. 27. — This afternoon the soldiers quitted Faneuil Hall.

Oct. 29. — This day the troops went from Faneuil Hall into the barracks.

Oct. 31. — This morning very early a soldier of Colo. Dalrymple's regiment was shot for desertion.

Nov. 3. — This morning Colo. Kerr's regiment was reviewed by the General.

Nov. 7. — [General Gage and other officers-dine at Cambridge at Mr. Inman's.]

Nov. 8. — I paid Genl. Gage a visit this morning, who received me very politely and agreeably.

Nov. 9. — Tis reported that the Commissioners [of the Customs] came to town this day. I saw one of them, Mr. Robinson.

Nov. 10. — This morning Colo. Pomroy arrived with part of the Irish regiments No. 64 and 65.

Nov. 13. — Sunday. The Viper man of war arrived, Capt. Lyndsay,[1]

---

[1] Robert or John Linzee.

from Hallifax. The Commissioners and their officers all at church this day, and the first time they have appeared in publick. Dr. Catherwood arrived in the Romney man of war, Capt. Connor, from Hallifax; in her the Commodore and lady, also Lord Wm. Campbell, and Capt. Goold. The Doctor gives the Commodore Hood a great character.

Nov. 24. — General Gage and family went out of town this morning. I took my leave of the General, who behaves very politely, &c.

Dec. 1. — Thanksgiving day. I paid a visit to Lord Wm. Campbell at Mr. Boutineau's, who was going on board.

Dec. 5. — Be it remembered that Sir Thos. Rich of the Senegall pressed all Capt. Dashwood's hands.

Dec. 15. — Capt. McNeal arrived from Quebec, who brought me a bill on the Commissioners of the Customs. I attended with Capt. Watts from twelve till almost three on their high mightinesses; this behavior is not only very insolent, but not to be born, and for which they may hear more about.

Jan. 10, 1769. — When I came home [in the evening] I found the Rev^d Mr. Walter, with whom I had two hours' conversation on the times.

Jan. 19. — Queen's Birth Day. Three regiments under arms in the Common, 14th, 29th, 64th; they made a fine appearance. Spent the evening at the Assembly for the first time; too much confusion.

March 13. — Town meeting. I desired my friends not to vote for me as Selectman, and in consequence was not chose, but Mr. Jonathan Mason was chose in my room. In the afternoon I went to town meeting. Mr. Saml. Adams affair came on, and the prayer of his petition granted, which appears to me to be a very wrong step in the town, and what they I am afraid will repent.

April 12. — Some letters of Govr Bernard to the Earl of Hillsborough are sent over by Mr. Bollan, which makes great noise and censure.

April 16. — I paid a visit to the Generall this forenoon.

April 19. — I paid a visit to Commodore Hood this morning.

April 24. — This afternoon Mr. Hooper of Marblehead came to town, and bring the melancholly account of Lieut. Panton being killed in endeavoring to press some hands of Mr. Hooper's brigg, Capt. Poor, from Cadiz.

May 23. — This day a special court of admiralty sat at the Court House on the tryall of a man that killed Lieut. Panton of the Rose. They consisted of the Governour, Commodore Hood, Lieut.-Governour, the Secretary, Judge Auchmooty, Robt. Trail, Esq., Collector of Portsmouth, and Mr. Nutting, Collector of Salem; they adjourned to Thursday. The lawyers that pleaded for the Crown, the King's attorney, Mr. Fitch his assistant; for the prisoner, James Otis, Esq., and John Adams, Esq.

June 14. — This day Power and others were on tryal for their conduct on board the Rose man of war; their behaviour was very courageous, and I think very right.

July 8. — When I came home [in the afternoon] I found Capt. Robt. Lyndsay at our house, being arrived in the Viper sloop of war from So. Carolina, his brother Capt. John Lyndsay, and Mr. Harry Hood.

Aug. 1. — This forenoon Capt. Thompson in the Rippon man of war for England, and Gov. Bernard went home in him. The flagg hoisted on Liberty Tree; the bells ringing great joy to the people, a great bonfire in King Street, and on Fort Hill.

Aug. 4. — We sunk the box at my wharf this noon, and were very lucky. I attended the merchants' meeting this afternoon, who gave me a pretty tight lecture about the importation of some porter on board Jarvis. I wish the porter had not been imported, as tis like to make an uneasiness.

Aug. 14. — The Sons of Liberty met at Liberty Tree, and dined at Robinson's at Dorchester; they contained 139 carriages on their return. Mr. Hancock preceded the company, and Mr. Otis brought up the rear.

Sept. 5. — In the evening an affray happened at the Coffee House between Mr. Robinson the Commissioner and James Otis, Esq.; its said Otis is much bruised. [Otis brought an action against Robinson. Rowe was present at the trial, July 25, 1771, and records, July 26, the result, a verdict of £2000 sterling damages in favor of the plaintiff.]

Sept. 6. — I find the inhabitants greatly alarmed at the usage Mr. Otis met with; it is generally thought he was very rascally treated; this afternoon the sheriff took Mr. Brown, Esq., formerly of Salem, for being accessory in beating Mr. Otis; he was carried to Faneuil Hall, and examined before Justice Dana and Justice Pemberton, and followed by a great number of people, I believe about two thousand. Mr. Murray was there, and used roughly by the people.

Sept. 28. — Dined at his Honor the Lieut.-Governor's, with him, his two daughters, his two sons Thomas and Elisha, Mr. Harris, a gentleman from St. Christopher's, Mr. Birch and Mr. Paxton, two of the Commissioners, for the first time since their arrival I have been in their company, and which I did not know now.

Sept. 30. — This day the Custom House officers made a large seizure from Capt. John Homer, who I take to be a very honest, good man, and for which I am very sorry should happen at this time.

Oct. 3. — This morning the merchants met at Faneuil Hall to consider what measures should be taken about Capt. Bryant's cargo.

Oct. 4. — This day there was a town meeting, and the transactions are agreed to be printed to-morrow.

Oct. 28. — Mr. Mein's publication that appeared to-day has given great uneasiness, and this evening he was spoke to by Capt. Dashwood. Some people getting around, he got into Ezek¹ Price's office, and from there fired a pistoll and wounded a grenadier of the 29th regiment in the arm. Warrants were issued out to secure him, but he could not be found. In the evening a large mob assembled and got hold of one George Greyer, an informer, who they stript naked and pay'd [painted] him all over with tarr, and then covered him with feathers and put him in a cart and carried him through all the main streets of the town, huzzaing, &c., and at nine dismissed him; this matter occasioned much terror, &c., in some fearful people among the inhabitants. When this happened I was with the Possee.

1770. *Jan.* 1. — This afternoon the committee of merchants came to wait on me about Mr. Wm. Sheaffe's affair, Deacon Phillips, Wm. Dennie, Wm. Greenleaf, Mr. Mollineaux, and John Ruddock, Esq.

Jan. 9. — Dined at home with his Honor the Lieut.-Governour, his brother Foster Hutchinson, Esq., Col. Dalrymple, Capt. Caldwell, Mr. Nicholas Boylston, Mr. Inman, Mr. John Lane, and Mrs. Rowe.

Jan. 17. — Spent the afternoon at the merchants' meeting at Faneuil Hall, and part of the evening at the Coffee House. This day the Body of merchants visited Mr. Wm. Jackson.

Jan. 18. — The merchants met again this day, and the whole Body, as they are called, visited the sons of his Honor, Mr. Theophilus Lillie, Mr. John Taylor, Mr. William Jackson again, and Mr. Nat. Rogers. They adjourned untill to-morrow ten of clock.

Jan. 19. — The merchants met again to-day. Messrs. Hutchinson agreed to deliver up.

Jan. 23. — The Trade met again to-day at Faneuil Hall, which highly displeased the Lieut.-Governour, who sent the sheriff and ordered them to disperse, which they took no notice of. Colo. Dalrymple, I believe, ordered his regiment to keep under arms all night. The Body voted said Colo. Dalrymple should be cashiered.

Feb. 26. — This afternoon the boy that was killed by Richardson was buried, and I am very sure two thousand people attended his funerall.

March 3. — A quarrel between some of the 29th regiment and the ropemakers yesterday and to-day.

March 5. — Monday. This night the 29th regim^t on duty. A quarrel between the soldiers and inhabitants; the bells rung; a great number assembled in King Street. A party of the 29th under the command of Capt. Preston fired on the people; they killed five, wounded several others, particularly Mr. Edwd Payne in his right arm. Capt. Preston bears a good character; he was taken in the night and committed, also seven more of the 29th. The inhabitants are greatly enraged, and not without reason.

March 6. — Most all the town in uproar and confusion. The Govr and Council met. The cryer went about to warn a town meeting at eleven of clock. The inhabitants met at Faneuil Hall; they chose a respectable committee to wait on his Honor the Lieut.-Governour to desire the troops might be removed from the town. Upon which he consulted Colo. Dalrymple and Colo. Kerr. The Lieut.-Governour returned for answer that the 29th regiment should go to the Castle and the 14th regiment remain in town. Afternoon the inhabitants met at the Old South Meeting House; after some debate they unanimously voted not to accept the Lieut.-Governour's proposals, but chose another committee of seven to wait on him again and insist on all the troops being removed from the town, and without this is complied with, it would not be satisfactory to the inhabitants. The committee went and returned that his Honor would order both regiments to the Castle, and Colo. Dalrymple consented to it; this gave great joy to the inhabitants, and I believe a generall satisfaction, so that they went from the meeting very peaceably to their habitations.

March 7. — A military watch to-night.

March 8. — I attended the funeral of the four unhappy people that were killed on Monday last. Such a concourse of people I never saw before, — I believe ten or twelve thousand. One corps with their relations followed the other, and then the selectmen and inhabitants. A military watch again to-night.

March 9. — I went and paid a visit to Capt. Preston in goal, who I found in much better spirits than I expected. Military watch.

March 10. — Yesterday two companies of the 29th went to the Castle, and four companies more went this day; still a military watch.

March 12. — The remainder of the 29th went to the Castle this day; still a military watch.

March 15. — Spent the afternoon with the town committee, myself chairman, John Ruddock, Esq., Isaac Smith, Wm. Dennie and Mr. Timothy Fitch, at the Coffee House.

March 16. — Mr. Otis got into a mad freak to-night, and broke a great many windows in the Town House. All the 14th regiment are gone to the Castle, the last of them this day. Capt. Robson and Capt. Miller both sailed for London this forenoon, in Capt. Robson. Mr. Robinson, one of the Board of Commissioners, went passenger.

March 17. — This afternoon another of the unhappy sufferers was buried from Faneuil Hall. The General Court sitting at Cambridge, which will be the cause of a quarrell between the Lieut.-Governour and the House of Representatives.

March 18. — Colo. Dalrymple sent for me, and I paid him a visit. I was glad to find that Colo. Dalrymple was pleased with the answer to his letters by return of the express.

March 19. — Town meeting again to-day. The town voted a vessell to be hired to carry home dispatches, and Capt. Dashwood offered himself a candidate to carry them.

April 18. — Mr. Hancock was chosen Speaker of the House pro tempore, and negatived by the Lieut.-Governour. Colo. Warren was chose in his room and approved.

April 20. — I attended the meeting of the Trade, as it is called; they passed a vote I did not like. The infamous Richardson on tryall to-day.

April 21. — Richardson was found guilty by the jury. I attended the merchants' meeting this forenoon.

April 22. — This afternoon Mr. Otis behaved very madly, firing guns out of his window, that caused a large number of people to assemble about him.

April 24. — Capt. Scot brings an account of the repeal of the dutys on glass, oyl, paper, and painters' colours, but the duty on tea still remains. Tis said our Lieut.-Governour is made Governour; he negatived Cushing as Commissary Generall.

April 25. — Merchants' meeting. I attended. I was to my great mortification chose a committeeman.

April 26. — Attended merchants' meeting. I did not approve much of their proceedings; think them too severe.

May 16. — Yesterday Lord Drummond, Colo. Robinson, Colo. Dalrymple, and Jos. Goldthwait paid Mrs. Rowe and Sucky a visit.

May 17. — This morning the 29 regiment marched from the Castle to Providence.

May 18. — Just as I was going to bed there was a very great hallooing in the street, and a mob of upwards a thousand people; it seems they had got an informer, and put him in a cart covered with tarr and feathers, and so exhibited him thro' the streets.

June 4. — [Artillery election. Dinner at Faneuil Hall, where the Lieutenant-Governor, officers, and citizens were present.] Spent part of the evening with the House of Representatives at the Province House in drinking his Majesty's health. A great many gentlemen attended this publick mark of loyalty to his Majesty and family.

June 6. — Town meeting. Mr. John Adams was chose a member for the town.

June 14. — In the afternoon I paid the Lieut.-Governour a visit at his seat at Milton.

July 22. — Capt. Smith of the Nassau arrived from London, and gives an account of the prorogation of the Parliament, the 20th of May, without repealing the duty on tea. The people, I hope, will have virtue enough never to make use of it as long as the duty is demanded.

July 24. — This afternoon the Body, as they are called, met, and just before some of them proceeded through the streets with Dr. Young at their head, with three flags flying, drums beating, and a French horn. Thos. Baker carried one of them, for which he is much blamed by me.

going on since Nov. 28]; six of them were acquitted, and two were found guilty of manslaughter.

1771. *Jan.* 3. — [Concert and dance at Concert Hall. Colonel Dalrymple and officers of the navy present.]

Jan. 18. — [" The Queen's birthday, guns firing, jovial day"; dance at Concert Hall. Governor, Lieutenant-Governor, and officers of the army and navy present, "commissioners, all the best people in town: a general coalition, so that harmony, peace, and friendship will once more be established in Boston."]

Jan. 29. — Spent an hour with Mr. James Otis, who I found in a gloomy way.

March 14. — The Governour's [Hutchinson] commission read to-day, also the Lieut.-Governour [Andrew Oliver]; the company that waited on the Governour were gentlemen of reputation and the best fortunes. I dined at Mr. Geo. Erving's with him, Mrs. Waldo, Mr. John Erving, Mr. Inman, Mr. Porter the Comptroller of the Board, Mr. Robt. Hallowell, Comptroller of the Customs, and Mr. John Lane, and spent the evening at the Assembly, which was very brilliant.

March 15. — Afternoon the merchants met at the British Coffee House to prepare an address to the Governour. Present Richd Clark, Jos. Green, myself, John Erving, George Erving, Thos. Gray, Henderson Inches, Edwd Payne, Melatiah Bourne, Danl. Hubbard, Ezekiel Goldthwait, John Dennie, John Amory, and Solomon Davis, and spent the evening there with most of the same company.

March 18. — The merchants waited on his Excellency the Governour with their address; present 106.

April 3. — This day the General Court meets at Cambridge. The Governour was met by the gentlemen of Cambridge and escorted to the College, where there was an oration spoke in Latin by one of the students.

May 7. — I attended town meeting for the choice of representatives. Mr. Otis, Mr. Cushing, Mr. Saml. Adams, and Mr. Hancock were chose by a great majority.

June 16. — There were three seizures made, some tea at Plymouth, a schooner from St. Peters with brandy, wine, &c., another schooner that short entered her cargoe of molasses belonging to Mr. Forster of Cape Ann. These affairs give great uneasiness, and tis believed will raise the minds of the people.

June 17. — Another sloop was seized this day from St. Peters by Capt. Parker of the Boston man of war.

Aug. 17. — I am very busy in sending provisions off to the ships.

Sept. 4. — I dined on board the Beaver, Capt. John Linzee. The Beaver people made a seizure, for which I am sorry.

Nov. 16. — The printers of the Massachusetts Spy was sent for by the Govr and Council; they ordered the King's attorney to prosecute them.

1772. *Feb.* 5. — Mr. Goldthwait told us of a conference between him and Mollineux, very extraordinary, wanting Mr. G. to destroy Josiah Quincy and Benjn Kent.[1]

March 5. — A town meeting this morning; they adjourned to Dr. Sewall's meeting house, where there was an oration spoke by Dr. Warren on the memory of this day, two year; tis said upwards of four thousand people were present. . . . There was an exhibition at Mrs. Clappam's in King Street this evening; a great many spectators.

April 19. — James Otis came to town this day.

June 4. — [King's birthday celebrated by parade of Colonel Erving's regiment, the Grenadiers, and Major Paddock's company; visit to the Governor at the Council Chamber; and a ball at Concert Hall, attended by the admiral and other officers of the navy.]

June 24. — Wednesday, St. John's Day. Dr. Warren and his lodge walked in procession to Dr. Byles' church, where a sermon was preached by Mr. Saml. Fairweather. I dined with the lodges under my care at Brother Brackett's [names of the brethren given].

July 7. — Colo. Hancock turned out this forenoon with the Cadet company; they made a good figure and behaved very well throughout the whole of the exercise. The whole regiment appeared in the Common this afternoon, also Major Paddock's company; the whole behaved much better than usual.

October 31. — After dinner I rode over to Bracket's, where I spent an hour with Treasurer Gray, John Cotton, and we were joyned by James Otis, who [had] been to wait on Govr Hutchinson as a committee man from the Town of Boston.

Nov. 2. — I attended Mr. John Adams this morning about Colo. Lee's affair.

Nov. 16. — The Admirall sent for me this morning and told me about the fresh beef contract extending to New England, and demanded a supply for the ships at Rhode Island.

1773. *Feb.* 8. — This morning my brigg sailed for So. Carolina, Capt. Skimmer. Young Josiah Quincy went passenger.

March 5. — Dr. Church performed an oration at Dr. Sewall's meeting, the judges say to great acceptance. This evening an exhibition in Mrs. Clapham's balcony. A great concourse of people in King Street of all sorts, and a large number to remember the 5th of March, 1770, assembled at Mrs. Clapham's.

May 22. — Our commissioners returned home last night from the

---

[1] This record without further information is not intelligible. The "Josiah Quincy" must have been the "Junior," as the father retired from business to his estate in Braintree in 1756.

Congress of New York about the line, which was held at Hartford; they have adjusted the affair to the satisfaction of the Government. Present Gov*r*. Hutchinson, Genl. Brattle, Colo. Hancock and Major Hawley.

May 27. — Two of the Commissioners [of Customs] were very much abused yesterday when they came out from the publick dinner at Concert Hall, Mr. Hulton and Mr. Hallowell. W*m* Molineux, W*m* Dennie, Paul Revere and severall others were the principall actors.

June 4. — King's birthday, aged 35. Colo. Hancock and Company of Cadets, Major Paddock and artillery, Colo. Erving and the Regiment, Colo. Phipps and Company, all made their appearance in the Common; such a quantity or rather multitude of people as spectators I never saw before; they behaved very well.

July 25. — The Reverend Dr. Cooper's Meeting House, built new, was preached in for the first time this day.

Aug. 14. — This day the Sons of Liberty held their annual feast at Roxbury in the training field by John Williams'; there was upwards of four hundred that dined there.

Oct. 4. — I visited the Admirall this morning, and settled the accounts for July and August navy matters with Mr. Atkinson.

Oct. 25. — King's accession to the throne. The Cadets under arms. General muster at Cambridge.

Nov. 2. — This morning the Rev*d* Mr. Walter and Mr. Parker paid me a visit on affairs of our church. When I got abroad I found an advertisement stuck up at almost every corner as follows: —

"To the Freemen of this and the Neighbouring Towns, — Gen*m*, you are desired to meet at Liberty Tree this day at Twelve of Clock at noon, then and there to hear the Persons to whom the Tea shipped by the East India Company is consigned make a publick Resignation of their Office as Consignees upon Oath and also swear that they will re-ship any Tea that may be Consigned to them by said Company by the first Vessell sailing for London."

Boston, Nov. 3d, 1773. O. C., Secretary.

Nov. 3. — This day the inhabitants of the town are alarmed, occasioned by the advertisement of yesterday. The gentlemen to whom the tea was supposed to be consigned did not obey the summons and make their appearance at Liberty Tree, upon which the Sons of Liberty appointed a committee to go and wait of them to know their determination, upon which the committee with a large concourse of people went from Liberty Tree to the store of Mr. Rich*d* Clark and Sons at the bottom of King Street, where they found Mr. Rich*d* Clark, Mr. Benj*m* Faneuil, the Governour, two sons,[1] and Mr. Jos. Winslow of Marshfield,

---

[1] This probably means the Governor's two sons.

who are the gentlemen these teas are supposed to be consigned to.. There was several of their friends there with them, Colo. Hatch of Dorchester, Judge Lee of Cambridge, Mr. Nat. Cary, Mr. Tho' Laughton, Mr. John Winslow, and many others. Mr. Mollineaux, as chairman of this committee, then read to them a paper, and produced another which they required them to sign, &c. Mr. Richd Clark and the other gentlemen gave them for answer, they would not comply with their request, or words to that purpose; this was an unexpected answer to them, and has given them much displeasure. The principal people that accompanied Mr. Mollineux were as follows: Mr. Saml Adams, Mr. Wm Dennie, Mr. John Pitts, Col. Heath of Roxbury, Dr. Church, Dr. Warren, Dr. Young, Capt. Jno. Matchet, Capt. Hopkins, Nat Barber, Gabriel Johnnot, Ezek^l Chever, and about five hundred more as near as I could guess. I spent the evening at the Bunch of Grapes, Colo. Ingersoll, with Treas. Gray, Thos. Gray, James Warden, Nat Cary, Geo. Erving, Melatiah Bourn, Jos. Scot, Jos. Blanchard, Thos. Brattle, Tuthill Hubbard, Jos. Winslow, Jos. Goldthwait, John Cotton, Solo. Davis, Edwd Davis, Wm Davis, and Saml Quincy. The same piece was posted up this day as yesterday with this addition: "Show me the man that dare take this down."

Nov. 4. — The town very quiet this day. I dined at Bracketts on Boston Neck on turtle. . . . Spent the evening at the Possee. . . . Thos. Palmer Esq. had his ball to-night at the Concert Hall.

Nov. 5. — This day there is to be a town meeting. Mr. Palmer's ball was very brilliant; there were upwards of two hundred gentlemen and ladies. Very quiet for a Pope Night.

Nov. 6. — Town meeting again this forenoon.

Nov. 11. — The geese flew to the s^{o}ward yesterday.

Nov. 12. — The Govr sent Colo. Hancock an order for him to hold his company in readiness in case of any riot or tumult happening.

Nov. 17. — This morning Capt. Scot arrived from London; he brings advice that Hall, Loring, Coffin, and Bruce are to bring the tea from the East India Company. This a measure that is generally disapproved, and will remain the great occasion of disagreement between England and America.

Nov. 18. — Last night a considerable body of people paraded thro' the streets and attacked the house of Mr. Richd Clark. One of his family fired a gun from the house, but luckily did no hurt. They broke all his windows and window frames, but very little other damage. This morning a town meeting was called on this and the tea affair. Another committee chose. The gentlemen to whom the tea is consigned are still resolved to pursue such orders as they may receive.

Nov. 19. — This day the gentlemen to whom the tea is consigned petitioned the Governor and Councill relative their affairs.

Nov. 23. — The Governor and Councill met this morning on the tea matters.

Nov. 28. — Sunday. This morning was bro' me a threatening letter signed "Determined," which is on file. This agitated my mind, and I did not go to church. Capt. Hall arrived from London. Great noise about the tea on board of Capt. Hall.

Nov. 29. — This morning there were papers stuck up to the following purpose: " Friends, Brethren, Countrymen! That worst of Plagues, the Detestable Tea, ship'd for this Port by the East India Company, is now arrived in this harbour; the Hour of Destruction or manly Opposition to the Machinations of Tyranny stares you in the Face; every Friend to his Country, to himself and Posterity is now called upon to meet at Faneuil Hall at nine of clock, this Day (at which time the Bells will begin to Ring) to make a united and successful Resistance to this last worst and most Destructive Measure of Administration.

Boston, Nov. 29, 1773."

In consequence of the above notification about one thousand people met at Faneuil Hall, where they past a vote that they would at all events return this tea; from Faneuil Hall they adjourned to the Old South Meeting; afternoon they met again and adjourned untill the morning; there were in the meeting this afternoon ab' twenty-five hundred people as near as I could guess.

Nov. 30. — The Body met again this morning. The Gov' sent them a message advising them to depart at their perill. They took but little notice of the message; they met again this afternoon. I told him that I had purchased a cargo for Capt. Bruce' ship, that it was on the wharff, and that Capt. Bruce when he arrived would apply to the Body, and that I would endeavor to prevail on him to act with reason in this affair, and that I was very sorry he had any tea on board, — and which is very true, for it hath given me great uneasiness. I staid sometime at the meeting and was chose a committee man much against my will, but I dare not say a word. After dinner I was sent for by the Body by two messengers, John Ingersoll and Jos. Eyres. This was at the motion of Mr. Hancock. I wish he had omitted it.[1]

Dec. 1. — Met the Committee; present Sam Adams, Jno. Hancock, Jonathan Williams, myself.

Dec. 2. — Capt. Bruce arriv'd this morning from London.

Dec. 3. — This morning Capt. Bruce and I was sent for by the committee relative the tea on board him; they ordered him to Griffins Wharff and gave him the same directions as to Capt. Hall.

Dec. 8. — Capt. Coffin arrived in Nantasket Road with the smallpox, and part of the tea.

[1] A note of Rowe to Thomas and Elisha Hutchinson, other consignees of the tea, offering to advance money to them to pay the duty, will be found in "Diary and Letters" of Governor Hutchinson, i. 97.

Dec. 11. — This forenoon a committee was sent to me ab^t Bruce's ship, Dr. Warren, Wm Mollineux, John Pitts, to know when she would be unloaded and many other questions.

Dec. 16. — I being a little unwell staid at home all day and all the evening. The Body meeting in the forenoon adjourn'd untill afternoon. Broke up at dark. Several things passed between Mr. Rotch[1] and them. A number of people appearing in Indian dresses went on board the three ships Hall, Bruce, and Coffin; they opened the hatches, hoisted out the tea, and flung it overboard; this might, I believe, have been prevented. I am sincerely sorry for the event. Tis said near two thousand people were present at this affair.

Dec. 18. — The affair of destroying the tea makes great noise in the town; tis a disastrous affair, and some people are much alarmed. I can truly say I know nothing of the matter, nor who were concerned in it. I would rather have lost five hundred guineas than Capt Bruce should have taken any of this tea on board his ship.

Dec. 31. — The people of Charlestown collected what tea they could find in the town and burnt it in the view of a thousand spectators. There was found in the house of one Withington of Dorchester about half a chest of tea; the people gathered together and took the tea, brought it into the Common of Boston, and burnt it this night about eleven of clock. This is supposed to be part of the tea that was taken out of the ships and floated over to Dorchester.

1774. *Jan.* 7. — I paid Admiral Montagu a visit this morning, and found him very angry. I think without reason; be that as it may, if he is angry he may be pleased again, &c. I wish the good wishes of all mankind, and should esteem his favors; but as for his business, that don't give me any concern: he has taken it away without just cause.

Jan. 25. — John Malcom having done some violence to a man with a sword enraged the multitude that they took him and put him into a cart, tarr'd and feathered him, carrying through the principal streets of this town, with a halter about him, from thence to the gallows, and returned through the main street, making great noise and huzzaing. I did not see the number attending, but tis supposed by the people that did there were upwards of twelve hundred people; tis said that Malcom behaved with great fortitude and resolution. This was looked upon by me and every sober man as an act of outrageous violence, and when several of the inhabitants applyed to a particular justice to exert his authority and suppress the people and they would support him in the execution of his duty, he refused.

Jan. 26. — A great concourse of people were in quest of the infamous Richardson this night. They could not find him; very lucky for him.

[1] Rowe notes Francis Rotch's sailing for London Jan. 9, 1774, and return May 16.

Jan. 27. — The Generall Court met yesterday. The Governour's speech much admired.

Feb. 8. — The Judges of the Superior Court returned their answers to the House this day. Judge Trowbridge, Judge Ropes, Judge Foster Hutchinson, and Judge Cushing are willing to receive their salaries as granted them by the General Court, and relinquish their grants from the Crown. The Chief Justice, Peter Oliver, Esq., has received part of his money as salary granted him by the Crown already, and will not relinquish that grant; therefore the House voted his answer not satisfactory.

Feb. 11. — The House of Assembly passed several resolves against the conduct of the Chief Justice, Peter Oliver, Esq., which may be fully seen in Fleet's and Edes's and Gill's papers, and tis my opinion they 'l repent of their resolutions; they are in direct opposition to government at home.

Feb. 15. — The Superior Court met and adjourned untill this day week upon the account of the Chief Justice Peter Oliver. [Rowe gave a dinner to public characters, of whom Samuel Adams was one.]

Feb. 19. — Yesterday the whole House presented in a body a remonstrance to the Gov' relative to the Chief Justice Mr. Oliver.

Feb. 22. — This day the Superior Court adjourned to June, which has given great uneasiness.

Feb. 23. — I dined at home with the Honble. John Hancock, Esq., Major Joseph Hawley of Northampton, Mr. Robt. T. Paine of Taunton, Mr. John Pickering of Salem, Jedediah Prebble of Falmouth, Casco Bay, Mr. Isaac Lathrop of Plymouth, the Honble. Wm Sever of Kingston, Mr. Gorham of Charlestown, Mr. Inman, Mrs. Inman, Mrs. Rowe, and Geo. Inman.

March 5. — Mr. Hancock delivered an oration this day at Dr. Sewall's meeting-house to the greatest number of people that ever met on the occasion. I tryd to get in, but could not. Some gentlemen speak of the oration with great applause.

March 8. — Last evening the tea brought by Capt. Gorham in the Brigg Fortune was destroyed. This afternoon his Honor the Lieut.-Governour Andrew Oliver, Esq., was buried as follows. . . . Through some misunderstanding or blunder the gentlemen of the Councill did not attend this funeral, and but very few of the House of Representatives. There was, after Colo. Hancock's company had fired and the funerall over, as the relatives were retiring, some rude behaviour.

March 12. — Capt. Solo. Davis and I had a few words about trifles; he was wrong. I took him up a little too quick. I am sorry, as I believe him honest but too volatile.

April 8. — I rose early and went down to my wharff, and there had a long conversation with Admiral Montagu.

April 17. — Mr. Henry Knox and Miss Lucy Flucker paid us a visit. [They were married June 16, 1774.]

April 18. — This day the Admirall made his son George Montagu Post, and gave him command of the Foye in the room of Capt. Jordan, who has liberty to go home; he also made old Mr. Thornborough master and commander. The court martial set this day to try Lieut. Rogers on board the Active [names of members of the court]. The result we shall soon know.

April 24. — The Post, Mr. Peter Mumpford, brings an account that the tea ship is arrived from Antigua to New York last Monday at Sandy Hook.

April 30. — This evening the York paper brings an account of the destruction of eighteen boxes of tea belonging to Capt. Chambers.

May 10. — The annual town meeting; the four old representatives were chosen, Saml. Adams, John Hancock, Wm Phillips, and Thos. Cushing; they were almost unanimously chosen. The Harmony, Capt. Shayler, arrived from London, and brings the severest Act ever was penned against the town of Boston.

May 13. — Town meeting this day, relating to the distressing situation of this town, occasioned by a late Act of Parliament [Boston Port Bill] for blocking up the harbour of Boston, which is and will [be] a great evill; at present there is no describing the circumstances. The Lively man of war, Capt. Bishop, is arrived this day and brought out Generall Gage, our new Governour. God grant his instructions be not severe, as I think him to be a very good man.

May 14. — Spent most part of the day with the town's committee at the Representatives' room. Present Saml. Addams, myself, John Addams, Thos. Cushing, Wm Phillips, Henderson Inches, William Mollineux, Dr. Warren.

May 16. — I spent both parts of the day with the town's committee at the Town House. Present Mr. Samuel Adams, John Adams, Esq., Josiah Quincy, jun^r., Esq., Wm Phillips, Esq., Mr. Henderson Inches, Mr. William Mollineux, Thos. Cushing, Esq., and myself. Capt. Hall arrived from London; in him came passengers, our assistant the Rev. Mr. Parker, Mr. Francis Rotch, and Mr. William Palfry.

May 17. — This morning Generall Gage, our new Governour, landed from the Castle after having breakfasted with Admirall Montagu on board the Captain man of war; he was saluted by the Castle and the Captain man of war, and received at the Long Wharff by Colo. Hancock's Company of Cadets. The Regiment was under arms in King Street. The Company of Grenadiers made a good appearance. Capt. Paddock's Company of artillery and Col. Phipps' Company of Guards were also under [arms] in King street; he came to the Town House, had his commission read by the Secretary, and took the usual oaths; from thence he was escorted to Faneuil Hall, where a good dinner by his Majesty's Council. There were but very few gentlemen of the town asked to dine there.

May 18. — I waited on Generall Gage this morning, who received me very cordially. The town met by adjournment this day. I was so busy I could not attend.

May 24. — The merchants met at the Town House on business of importance.

May 29. — The Admirall has now stationed all his ships [stations given].

May 30. — I paid the Generall a visit this morning. Town meeting, nothing done but harangue.

May 31. — The Minerva, Capt. Calahan, is gone below to take in Gov' Hutchinson, his son Elisha Hutchinson, and his daughter, Miss Peggy Hutchinson, who are going passengers, as is Miss Polly Murray.

June 1. — This is the last day any vessell can enter this harbour until this fatall Act of Parliament is repealed. Poor unhappy Boston. God knows only thy wretched fate. I see nothing but misery will attend thy inhabitants.

June 2. — I met the gentlemen merchants at the west side of the Court House in Boston. While we were in the meeting Capt. Williamson arrived at Marblehead from Bristoll and brought with him another Act of Parliament for the better regulating the Province of the Massachusetts Bay, which Act strikes the very Charter granted to this Province by King William and Queen Mary, and is, or will be, productive with many evils to the advancement of this his Majesty's Province, and sour the minds of most of the inhabitants thereof. I am afraid of the consequences that this Act will produce. I wish for harmony and peace between Great Britain, our mother country, and the Colonies; but the time is farr off. The people have done amiss, and no sober man can vindicate their conduct, but the revenge of the ministry is too severe.

June 3. — Spent the evening at Deacon Jones' with the following merchants: John Amory, Jonathan Amory, Saml. Barrat, Henderson Inches, John Timmins, Eben' Storer, Wm Whitwell, Edw. Payne, Henry Bromfield, and myself. We adjourned untill Monday evening.

June 6. — Artillery election. Brigg' Brattle did the honors of the day in the absence of his Excellency Governor Gage.

June 7. — There was a grand ball at Salem last evening as an entertainment to Generall Gage, his officers, the Commissioners of the Customs, and many others.

June 8. — The committee of merchants waited on Genl. Gage with their address, Treas. Gray, Thos. Gray, Jno. Erving, Geo. Erving,

Richd. Letchmere, John Timmins, Jos. Winslow, Frank Green, James Forrest, James Anderson.

June 10. — The transports with the 4th Regiment are arrived from Southampton this morning.

June 12, *Sunday.* — After church I walked round the wharffs; tis impossible to describe the distressed situation of this poor town, not one topsail merchantman to be seen.

June 14. — This is the last day any vessell can depart this harbour. Boston, thy fate is very distressing. The fourth Regiment landed this morning, and pitched their tents in the Common by the pound, a number of spectators to see them.

June 15. — The forty-third Regiment landed this morning, and pitched their tents in the Common near the workhouse on that plain. This evening the tradesmen of the town met to consult on the distress of this place. There were upwards of eight hundred at this meeting; they did nothing, being much divided in sentiment.

June 16. — I went this morning to see my kinsman Jacob Rowe, who I found very ill and very dangerous. After dinner I spent an hour with John Adams and Josiah Quincy, jun^r. [Jacob Rowe (not John's brother) died June 20, and was buried in John Rowe's tomb under Trinity Church the 22d.]

June 17. — A generall town meeting this forenoon; they chose me moderator. I was much engaged, and therefore did not accept. The people at present seem very averse to accommodate matters. I think they will repent of their behaviour sooner or later. The Governor dissolved the Assembly this day. The General Court chose a committee of five to go to the Generall Congress, James Bowdoin, John Adams, Sam. Adams, the Speaker, and Mr. Paine of Taunton.

June 27. — Town meeting; the hall so full they adjourned to the Old South Meeting House. The debates were for and against the Committee of Correspondence, very warm on both sides; it lasted all day, and adjourned until to-morrow 10 of clock. The speakers in behalf of the committee were Saml. Adams, Josiah Quincy, jun^r, Dr. Warren, Dr. Young, Wm Mollineux, Benj. Kent. The speakers against the behaviour of the committee were Treas^r Gray, Thos. Gray, Saml. Elliot, Saml. Barrat, John Amory, Edw. Paine, Francis Greene, Ezek. Goldthwait.

June 28. — The town met again at the Old South Meeting. The debates very warm on both sides. I think [the committee] are wrong in the matter. The merchants have taken up against them; they have in my opinion exceeded their power; and the motion was put that they should be dismissed. The gentlemen that made and supported this motion could not obtain their vote; the majority were four to one against them. This affair will cause much evill, one against the other. I wish for peace in this town. I fear the consequences.

July 1. — [The Preston man of war, transports and soldiers, with Admiral Graves and Lord Percy arrive.]

July 4. — The 38 Regiment landed this day, and pitched their tents in the Common. I paid Admirall Montagu a visit this morning.

July 5. — The 5th Regiment landed this day, and pitched their tents in the Common. Admirall Montagu's Lady, and Miss Sophie Montagu paid us a visit this morning, and took leave of us, being just on their departure for England.

July 7. — The Captain man of war, with the Admirall on board, saluted Admirall Graves; but the wind dyed away; they did not sail. The Generall visited the troops in the Common this forenoon.

July 8. — I heard of the bad behaviour of the people at Marlborough; its said the Speakmans were concerned; if it proves so, they have not only behaved ill, but contrary to my sentiments, and forfeited my regard in future for them.

July 12. — Capt. Dove arrived from So. Carolina at Salem, with rice as a present from sundry gentlemen there for this place.

July 14. — This day a fast is recommended by some of the ministers on account of the miserable situation of this town. I cannot reconcile this measure, and should much rather the people would do justice, and recommend the payment for the tea instead of losing a day by fasting.

July 18. — Heard of my old friend Capt. Thos. Gerry of Marblehead being dead.

July 20. — This day is the annuall Commencement Day, but the distressed situation of the Town and Province prevents it being kept publick as usual. I paid a visit to Generall Gage this morning, who received [me] very friendly.

July 25. — After dinner my brother Jacob set out for Quebeck. [He had arrived in Boston March 31.]

July 27. — A quarrell happened last night between some of the town's people and some officers of the Army. Town meeting yesterday. I did not attend.

Aug. 7. — The Scarborough man of war arrived yesterday from England; she left Plymouth the last port. A letter from Sucky by Mr. Hutt, who is lieutenant of the Scarborough. . . . I wrote the Generall [Gen. Gage, then at Salem] a few lines by Mr. Humphreys.

Aug. 7, 9, 10, 17. — [Arrival of vessels with troops, and appointments to civil offices under the late Act of Parliament.]

Aug. 12. — I waited on Generall Gage, Lord Percy, and Genl. Piggot with Major Clark.

Aug. 21. — A vessell arrived from Falmouth at Marblehead brings advice of Govr Hutchinsons arrivall in England, having a short passage from hence in Capt. Callahan.

Aug. 22. — A report that Daniel Leonard, Esq., one of the Counsellors at Taunton, was obliged to leave the town of Taunton. [Names of persons sworn in as members of the Council.]

Sept. 1. — This morning a letter was picked up wrote by Genl Brattle to Genl Gage, and the Genl. in consequence sent a party of two hundred men under the command of Colo. Mattison, and took the gun powder belonging to the Province from the arsenall on Quarry Hill, and brought it from thence in the transport boats to the Cassell. This letter has exasperated the country people against Brattle, so that he now takes refuge in Boston.

Sept. 2. — A great number of people from the country are collected at Waltham, Watertown, and Cambridge, occasioned as tis reported from the behaviour of Genl Brattle. The people seem to be frightened and afraid of its consequence. The Generall has reinforced the entrance at the Neck. Commissioner Hallowell has been insulted in his way through Cambridge; he fled for shelter to this town. This evening appeared a flimsy recantation from Genl Brattle.

Sept. 3. — The people of Cambridge mostly dispersed, and gone home. The Generall sent four field pieces to Boston Neck.

Sept. 4, *Sunday.* — Mr. Parker read prayers and preached. Severall gentlemen of distinction were at our church, Peter Oliver, Esq., Chief Justice, Judge Brown of Salem, Jona. Sewall, Esq., Attorney Generall, Wm Pepperell, Esq., and a great many others, too many to particularize.

Sept. 7. — The Generall has doubled the guards at the Neck, and I believe designs to fortify it.

Sept. 9. — This morning a soldier of the 65th regiment, which had three times deserted, was shot on the Common.

Sept. 10. — The 59th regiment came from Salem and encamped on the west side of Boston Neck.

Sept. 14, *Wednesday.* — Church convention. I went to Chapell. Dr. Caner read prayers, and Mr. Sergeant of Cambridge preached a sensible, short sermon on the occasion. The Generall and his aid de camps, the Admirall and lady, and the Capt. of the Preston, with the navy officer of the day, the Commissioners, many of the Councill, the High Sheriff, and many other gentlemen and ladies attended. This night some of the officers of the navy came and spiked up the guns of the North Battery, a ridiculous manœuvre.

Sept. 22. — This day is the anniversary of his Majesty's accession to the throne. I went to the Councill Chamber with the Governour, Admirall, and many other gentlemen to drink the King's health and many other loyal toasts.

Oct. 11. — A number of deputys met at Concord this day. Capt. Callahan arrived from London at Salem, severall passengers, among the rest Geo. Inman.

Feb. 27. — I paid Admirall Graves a visit this forenoon. Colo. Lessly has been to Salem on an expedition and returned again.

March 6. — This day Dr Warren delivered an oration in Dr Sewall's Meeting. I did not hear him.

March 9. — This morning a country fellow who had bought a gun from one of the soldiers was published by them in the modern taste of tarring and feathering, and carried in a cart through the main streets of the town.

March 15. — This day an oration was delivered by a dirty scoundrell from Mrs. Cordis' balcony, wherein many characters were unfairly represented and much abused, and mine among the rest.

March 16. — This day is kept by many people as a Publick Fast, which gives great umbrage to a great many people which do not pay any regard to it, and I think they are not right, because they say the order does not originate under the direction of good government; yet it can [do] no harm.

March 25. — Afternoon the Generall sent for me to see a letter I received from Thos. Griffith.

April 16, *Sunday*. — I dined at home with Mrs. Rowe, Geo. Inman, and Jack Rowe. After dinner I went down Clarks Wharff to meet Capt. Linzee and Sucky, who arrived from Spithead and Falmouth in the Falcon sloop. I brought them home and their little son Saml Hood Linzee.

April 17. — [The Inmans and Linzees guests at dinner.] Our house full of visitors all day. Gen. Robinson and Major Moncrieff came to town from New York.

April 18, *Tuesday*. — I dined at home with Capt. Linzee, Mrs. Linzee, Mrs. Rowe, and George Inman, and spent the evening at home with them and Jack Rowe. [Capt. Linzee and Mrs. Linzee are recorded as dining every day at Rowe's, from their arrival until they left Boston May 1, except that on April 19th only her name appears.]

April 19. — Last night the Grenadiers and Light Companies belonging to the several regiments in this town were ferry'd over Charles River, and landed on Phipps farm in Cambridge, from whence they proceeded on their way to Concord, where they arrived early this day. On their march they had a skirmish with some country people at Lexington.

The First Brigade, commanded by Lord Percy, with two pieces of artillery, set off from this town this morning about 10 of clock, as a reinforcement, which with the Grenadiers and Light Infantry made about eighteen hundred men. The people in the country had notice of this movement; early in the night alarm guns were fired thro' the country and expresses sent off to the different towns, so that very early this morning large numbers from all parts of the country were assembled.

A generall battle ensued, which from what I can learn was supported with great spirit on both sides, and continued untill the King's troops got back to Charlestown, which was near sunset. Numbers are killed and wounded on both sides. Capt. Linzee and Capt. Collins in two small armed vessells were ordered up Charles River to bring off the troops to Boston, but Lord Percy and Generall Smith thought proper to encamp on Bunker's Hill this night; this unhappy affair is a shocking introduction to all the miseries of a Civil War. I dined at home with the Rev^d Mr. Parker, Mrs. Linzee, Mrs. Rowe, and George Inman, and spent the evening at home with Mr. Inman, Mrs. Linzee, Mrs. Rowe, George Inman, and Jack.

April 20. — The Generall sent some more troops to Charlestown last night and this morning, so that Lord Percy and the troops under his command returned to town. This night some people, about two hundred, attacked Capt. Linzee in the armed schooner a little below Cambridge bridge, and he gave them a warm reception, so that [they] thought proper to retreat with the loss of some men. I dined at home with Capt. Collins of the Nautilus, Capt. Linzee, the Rev^d Mr. Parker, Mr. Inman, Mrs. Rowe, Geo. Inman, and spent the evening at home with Mr. Inman, Capt. Linzee, Mrs. Linzee, Richd Green, Mrs. Rowe, Geo. Inman, and Jack.

Tis said many thousands of country people are at Roxbury and in the neighbourhood. The people in town are alarmed, and the entrenchments on Boston Neck double-guarded. Mrs. Linzee dined at the Admirall's.

April 21. — The reinforcement that was sent to Charlestown by the Genl are returned too, and the 64th Regim^t that was at the Castle are now in Boston Town House. All business at an end, and the communication stop'd between the town and country. No fresh provision of any kind brought to this market, so that Boston is in a most distressed condition. I dined at home with Capt. Linzee, Mrs. Rowe, Mrs. Linzee, Mr. Inman, and Geo. Inman.

This afternoon severall gentlemen met with the Selectmen to consult on our situation, and chose a committee to draft a memoriall to Genl Gage, viz.: the Selectmen, James Bowdoin, Henderson Inches, Alex. Hill, Edward Payne, and Jos. Barrell; they adjourned until tomorrow ten of clock. I spent the evening at home with Mr. Inman, Mrs. Linzee, Mrs. Rowe, and Geo. Inman.

April 22. — The same company met and reported, upon which the inhabitants were called together; after much debate and some amendments they passed two votes, which were presented to the Generall by the same committee, and on delivery they asked the Generall to grant their prayer; he in some measure complyed, but made some other proposalls.

I dined at home with Capt. Linzee, Mrs. Linzee, Mr. Inman, Geo. Inman, and Jack Rowe, also Mrs. Rowe, and spent the evening at home with the same company. Mr. Nicholls sent Jack home last night, and broke up his school.

April 23. — The inhabitants met again this morning, and after some debate they came into the Generall's measures, which was to deliver up their arms to be deposited in the hands of the Selectmen; and such of the inhabitants as had a mind to leave the town might go with their effects. This evening news was brought that Capt. Brown was stop'd at Charlestown in his way by the country people.

April 24. — I rose very early, and got away Mr. Nun, John Inman, Mr. Sparks, Thos. Knights, Jos. Taylor, and John Head on board Mr. Sheriff's sloop for Salem. Between one and two Capt. Brown got to town. I soon despatched him. This day the inhabitants carried in their arms; the number 2674.

April 26. — John Inman is come to town, and tells me that my brigg Sucky sailed from Marblehead yesterday towards night; in her went the following passengers [names given]. The Admirall's lady paid Mrs. Linzee a visit this morning. Mr. Sheriff sent upwards of 40 sheep into our pasture this day.

April 27. — The General has given leave for all people to leave the town that chooses with their effects.

April 28. — This day I apply'd to get a pass to go out with my effects, but could not prevail.

May 1. — Capt. Linzee and Sucky and little Sam Hood sailed this morning in the Falcon sloop.

May 2. — The post is in; bad news from New York. Dr. Wm Samuel Johnson and Col. Wallcot are come to town on special business with the Generall from the Colony of Connecticut.

May 3. — Mr. Inman went to the lines to see Mrs. Inman; he had some conversation with her.

May 5. — The inhabitants flocking out of town. Some transports arrived from Hallifax with four companies of the 65th Regiment.

May 10. — William Vassall and all his family, together with Tim^o Fitch and family, Thos. Brattle, and many others went off this morning.

May 13. — I paid a visit to Genl. Robertson, where I found Colo. Abercrombie, Major Goldthwait, and Doct^r Mallet.

May 17. — [Fire broke out in the barracks of the 65th regiment on Treat's wharf, destroying 33 stores on Dock Square.]

May 21. — A party was sent under the command of Mr. Innis of the 43^d to Grape Island to bring off some cattle and hay; the country people being very numerous kept a brisk fire on them, so that they were obliged to return without effecting their design. One marine wounded. Two transports from Deptford, with recruits, and one with marines from Plymouth, arrived this day.

May 24. — [Arrival of troops.]

May 25. — The Cerberus man of warr, Capt. Chad, arrived from Spithead; in this ship the Generalls Burgoyne, How, and Clynton came passengers.

May 28. — A continual firing all night on Norten's [Noddle's] Island between the Provincialls and marines and sailors. Severall marines and sailors killed and wounded, and tis supposed the Provincials lost many.

May 29. — Twenty sheep and lambs have been killed this night in my pasture.

May 30. — Last night the country people burnt one house and severall barns on Norten's [Noddle's] Island, and the dwelling house and store this forenoon. Our two girls Peggy and Becky went away this day.

[Vol. XII. of the Diary, pp. 2007–2077, is missing, and inside the cover of Vol. XIII. is written "from June to December is mislaid or taken away out of my store."]

Dec. 25, *Christmas Day.* — Mr. Walter read prayers, and Mr. Parker preached a very good sermon from the 2^d chap. St. Luke's Gospell & 14th verse. The money gathered for the use of the poor of this church amounted to sixty dollars.

Dec. 27. — I dined at home with Capt. Linzee, Mrs. Linzee, little Saml. Hood Linzee, who is two years old this day.

Dec. 30. — [Arrival of ships with troops.] The Scarborough, Capt. Barclay, and severall transports sailed to-day on a secret expedition.

Dec. 31. — Thus endeth the year 1775, a most fatal year for this part of America. The Niger man of war, Capt. Talbot, is arrived in Nantasket Road, and has brought the King's speech, dated the 26 October.

1776. *Jan.* 7, *Sunday.* — Capt. Linzee behaved very cruelly to me; I shall not forget it.[1] [Rowe and Linzee were, however, much together at Rowe's and Inman's till Capt. Linzee sailed.]

Jan. 12. — I paid Admiral Shouldham a visit this morning, who is a genteel man, and received me politely.

Jan. 14. — I staid at home and dined at home with Capt. Linzee, Mrs. Linzee, Mr. Inman, Mrs. Inman, Geo. Inman, Mrs. Rowe, and Jack Rowe.

Jan. 18. — Mrs. Linzee and George paid us a visit, and took their leave, perhaps forever. [War ship arrived.]

Jan. 20. — This day the Falcon, Capt. Linzee, sailed. He took with him Mrs. Linzee, little Sam, and Hannah. I sincerely wish their prosperity and happiness. With the Falcon sailed the Mercury; in her

---

[1] Pages of the Diary covering Jan. 8, 9, 15, and 16, torn out.

March 5. — This morning we perceived a battery erected on the hill on Dorchester Neck. This has alarmed us very much. About 12 the Generall sent off six regiments; perhaps this day or tomorrow determines the fate of this truly distressed place. All night both sides kept a continuall fire. Six men of the 22nd are wounded in a house at the South End; one boy lost his leg. A very severe storm; it blew down my rail fences, both sides the front of the house.

Mar. 6. — This morning the country people have thrown a strong work on another place on the Neck at Dorchester Neck. Gen'l Howe has ordered the troops ashore again, and tis now out of doubt that Gen. Howe will leave this town with his troops, &c., which has put the inhabitants of this town into great disorder, confusion, and much distress. The firing has ceased this day.

Mar. 7. — The troops and inhabitants very busy in getting all the goods and effects on board the shipping in the harbour; tis impossible to describe the distresses of this unfortunate town. I dined and spent the evening at home with my dear Mrs. Rowe, Mr. Inman, and Jack Rowe. Genl Robinson paid me a visit.

Mar. 8. — My situation has almost distracted me. John Inman, Archy McNeil, and Duncan are determined to leave me. God send me comfort in my old age. I try to do what business I can, but am disappointed, and nothing but cruelty and ingratitude falls to my lot. I spent the day with my dear Mrs. Rowe, Richard Green, and John Haskins.

March 9. — I dined at home with the Rev^d Mr. Parker, Mrs. Rowe, and Jack, and spent the evening at the Possee. This day Genl Robinson pressed the ship Minerva into the service; nothing but hurry and confusion, every person striving to get out of this place. A great deal of firing on both sides this night.

March 10, *Sunday.* — Capt. Dawson is returned with two vessells; he has had a severe brush with four privateers. A proclamation came out from Genl How this day, a very severe one on some people. John Inman went on board this day with his wife; he has in his possession three watches of mine — sundry pieces of checks which was to be made into shirts. Jos. Goldthwait [and] Mrs. Winslow went on board this day; he has carried off Capt. Linzee's horse without paying for him.

March 11. — This morning I rose very early and very luckily went to my warehouse; when I came there I found Mr. Crean Brush with an order and party from the Gen'l, who were just going to break open the warehouse, which I prevented by sending for the keys, and opening the doors. They took from me to the value of twenty two hundred and sixty pounds sterling, according to the best calculation I could make, in linnens, checks, cloths, and woollens. This party behaved very insolently and with great rapacity, and I am very well convinced exceeding their orders to a great degree. They stole many things and plundered my store. Words cannot describe it. This party consisted of Mr. Blasswitch, who was one of the Canceaux people, Mr. Brush, the provost, Mr. Cunningham, a refugee, Mr. Welch the provost deputy, a man named Hill, and about fifteen soldiers, with others. I remained all day in the store, but could not hinder their destruction of my goods. This day I got a piece of bread and one draft of flip. I spent the evening at home with Mr. Parker, Richᵈ Green, Mr. Warner of Portsmouth, who assisted me very much, with Mrs. Rowe and Jack Rowe. They are making the utmost speed to get away, and carrying ammunition, cannon, and everything they can [carry] away, taking all things they meet with, never asking who is owner or whose property, making havoc in every house and destruction of all kinds of furniture. There never was such destruction and outrage committed any day before this. Many other people have suffered the same fate as me, particularly Mr. Samˡ Austin, Mr. John Scolly, Capᵗ Partridge, Capt. Dashwood, Mr. Cyrus Baldwin, the Widow Newman.

Mar. 12. — A continual fire from both sides this night. They are hurrying off all their provisions and destroying and mangling all navigation; also large quantitys of salt and other things they heave into the sea and scuttle the stores. The inhabitants are greatly terrified and alarmed for fear of greater evils when the troops leave this distressed place. I got Crean Brush receipt for the goods taken from me, but don't expect much good from it, the severall gentlemen say they will be my friend in this affair.

March 13. — I have staid at home most part of this day. The confusion still continues, and plundering of houses, &c., increasing. Genᵗ Robinson paid me a visit and eat a morsell of provisions, together with Richᵈ Green, Mrs. Rowe, and Jack Rowe. The sailors from the ships have broke open my stores on my wharff and plundered them; this was done at noon this day. This morning a house was burnt at the North End, whether set on fire on purpose or from accident seems uncertain. A considerable number of cannon fired in the night from both sides. The country people throwing up more entrenchments, &c., on Dorchester Neck.

March 14. — This night much damage has been done to many houses and stores in this town, and many valuable articles stolen and destroyed. Stole out of Wᵐ Perry's store a quantity of tea, rum, and sugar, to the value of £120 sterling. Mr. Sam. Quincy's house broke and great destruction, the Revᵈ Mr. Walter's, also the Revᵈ Dr. Caner's and many others.

Mar. 15. — This night my store on the Long Wharff broke open and almost a hhd. of sugar and a hogshead of ware stole. Twas expected the troops would have embarked this night, but they still remain in town; I dined at home with Gen¹ Robertson, Colo. Clark, Rich⁴ Green, an officer of the 5ᵗʰ reg¹, Mrs. Rowe, and Jack Rowe; after dinner, Cap¹ Haskins gave me notice that several officers were in Mrs. Hooper's house, committing violence and breaking everything left; they broke a looking glass over the chimney which cost twenty guineas — such barbarous treatment is too much for the most patient man to bear. I spent the evening at home with Rich. Green, Mrs. Rowe, and Jack Rowe.

Mar. 16. — The troops are getting everything in order to depart. My store on Loug Wharff broke open again this night; the behaviour of the soldiers is too bad, tis almost impossible to believe it. Two officers of the 5ᵗʰ came to me for wine; they wanted to be trusted; I refused them; since I have heard nothing, only they damned me and swore they would take it by force; one of them named Russell of the 5ᵗʰ Regiment, the other I don't know.

Mar. 17, *Sunday.* — St. Patrick's day. The Provincials are throwing up a battery on Nook Hill on Dorchester Neck, which has occasioned much firing this night. This morning the troops evacuated the town, and went on board the transports at and about Long Wharff; they sailed and got most part of them into King Road. About noon Gen¹ Putnam and some troops came into town to the great joy of the inhabitants that remained behind. I dined at home with Mr. Inman, Mrs. Inman, Mr. Warner, Mrs. Rowe, and Jack Rowe.

March 18. — Major Chester and Capt. Huntington lodged at our house. The town very quiet this night. Severall of my friends came to see me from the country.

Mar. 19. — Numbers of people belonging to Boston are daily coming in. Gen'l Washington and his retinue were in town yesterday. I did not hear of it; otherways should have paid my respects and waited on him. This afternoon the King's troops burnt the Block house at the Cassell and the Continental troops are throwing up a battery on Fort Hill; most all the ships are gone from King Road into Nantasket Road.

Mar. 20. — They burnt the barracks and houses at the Cassell this afternoon and destroyed everything they could on the island and blew up the fortifications all around it.

Mar. 22. — I dined at home with Generall Putnam, Generall Greene, Mr. Inman, Mrs. Inman, Mrs. Forbes, Mrs. Rowe, and Jack. After dinner Colo. Gridly, Mr. Chase, both Mr. Webbs, and severall other officers came to the house.

March 23. — I dined at Mr. Inman's with him, Mrs. Inman, Genl. Green, Mrs. Green, Tuthill Hubbard, Mrs. Forbes, Mr. Lowell (?) Mrs. Rowe, and Capt. Gilbert Speakman. Some fire below Nantasket Road; I take it to be a transport set on fire to destroy her.

Apr. 7, Sunday. — Mrs. Hooper came to town. She is in a most pitifull, distressed situation. The proprietors of Trinity Church met after church; present, twelve persons.

Apr. 8. — I attended the church meeting this morning, and was chose warden with Dan¹ Hubbard. Afternoon I went by invitation of Brother Webb to attend the funerall of the remains of Dr. Warren, and went accordingly to the Councill Chamber with a design to attend and walk in procession with the lodges under my jurisdiction, with our proper jewells and cloathing, but to my great mortification was very much insulted by some furious, hot persons — without the least provocation; one of brethren thought it most prudent for me to retire. I accordingly did so; this has caused some uneasy reflections in my mind, as I am not conscious to myself of doing anything prejudicial to the cause of America either by will, word, or deed. The corps of Dr. Warren was carried into Chapell. Dr. Cooper prayed and Mr. Perez Morton delivered an oration on the occasion. Dr. Warren's bearers were Genl. Ward, Genl. Fry, Col. Gridly, Dr Morgan, Mr. Moses Gill, and Mr. John Scolly. There was a handsome procession of the craft, with two companys of soldiers. There is a confirmation of Crean Brush and Wm. Jackson being taken, and also my negro fellow Adam.

Apr. 10. — I attended the proprietors of Trinity Church this morning on Mr. Parker's affairs. I see Mr. Jos. Wentworth, and had some conversation with him about Capt. Manley's capture. My worthy friend Benj. Green was taken out of this troublesome world this afternoon.

April 11. — This day Crean Brush and Wm Jackson were sent to Watertown under guard.

Apr. 12. — This morning came an account of Brymers brigg being taken in the bay by some whale boats under the command of Capt. Thatcher and carried into Hingham. Tis said the vessell taken by Thatcher is very valuable, and belongs to Bristol. Crean Brush and Wm. Jackson are brought to Boston.

April 13. — Martin Brimmer and Mr. Dalton of Newberry Port paid us a visit.

April 14, Sunday. — I staid at home all day, our church shut up. Mr. Parker gone to Newberry Port, and Mr. Bass expected to town, who disappointed him. I dined at home with Mr. Tristram Dalton, Mr. Warner, Mrs. Rowe, and Jack Rowe, and spent the evening at home with Mr. Inman, Mrs. Inman, Mrs. Rowe, Richd Green, Capt. Haskins, Mr. Warner, and Jack Rowe.

April 17. — Severall people taken up this day, and carried to gaol. Dr. Whitworth, his son, Wm Perry, one Edwards, and others.

April 18. — This morning the persons that were taken up were carried over to Dorchester and there examined by a court appointed by the Generall Court for that purpose; they examined Wm Perry and Edwards, and ordered them to gaol; the rest they kept all night there.

April 19. — Dr. Whitworth examined this day and admitted to bail.

May 1. — My dear little fellow and kinsman Jack Rowe taken very ill.

May 3. — Dr. Whitworth and son committed to close gaol.

May 4. — Jack very ill. Dr. Lloyd is afraid of him. The Justices adjourned until Wednesday week.

May 7. — Jack growing better, and I hope out of danger. Severall parties have been for severall days on Noddle's Island, throwing up breastworks, &c., for a fort.

May 8. — This morning Mr. Hammond's plough began to plough up the pasture. Two briggs, one from Cork, the other from the Western Islands, taken by Capt. Tucker in Manley's schooner, and carried into Lynn.

May 15. — [Justices met.]

May 17. — This is a Fast Day, appointed by the Continentall Congress throughout the Colonies. [Large British ship loaded with gunpowder and arms brought in, being taken by Capt. Mugford in a schooner from Beverly.]

May 21. — Bad news from Quebec. [Capt. Mugford attacked in Nantasket Road by boats from a man of warr, and killed.]

May 22. — The army from Quebec is retired from before it; the account imperfect.

May 23, 24, 27, 28. — [Town meetings, those on 23 and 24th to choose representatives.]

June 2 & 4. — [Dr. Church came to town and was confined.]

June 8, 9. — [Captures by privateers of provisions, and 95 soldiers, mostly Highlanders.]

June 11. — A flag of truce went from town on board the Renown, Mr. White of Marblehead and Mr. Martin Brimmer. Comm. Banks treated them very politely.

June 12. — A hand bill is sent about containing interesting [news] from the Continentall Army in Canada.

June 14. — An expedition went forward against the ships in Nantasket Road. Three separate bodies, one on Long Island, one on Pedricks [Petticks] Island, and another on Nantasket; they have driven the ships from Nantasket Road. Comm. Banks, its said, burnt the house on Georges Island and the house on the Light House Island.

June 15. — I have been very busy all this morning in finding out some persons that have wickedly and maliciously spread a false report about me, and have had them before Justice Hill, and have got the first of them to acknowledge it to be a lye, and she hath signed a declaration which I hope will satisfy and clear my innocence.

June 17, 18. — [British ships with Highlanders taken by privateers.]

June 22. — The Continentall affairs appear in Canada very unfavourable.

June 23–27, 29. — [Fleets of British ships in the bay, about four leagues from the Light House.]

June 25. — The Highland officers and soldiers are sent out of town to Mendon, Reading, and Lunenburg.

July 7. — [Captures by privateers, one of a vessel laden with 419 hogsheads of rum.]

July 11. — Young Shaw brought ten Indians from the Mirimiche and St. John's tribe; they are come to negotiate some business with the General Court, and are the headmen of their tribes. A report in town that Lord Howe has been spoke with; tis said his designs are to settle the present unhappy disputes that subsist between G. Britain and the United Colonies.

July 13, *Saturday*. — I attended the gentlemen sufferers by Crean Brush. Capt. Benj. Phillips was taken up this day. Tis said by Mr. Mumpford, the post, that Independence was declared the 4th instant at Philadelphia. A generall inoculation in this town for the small pox.

July 17. — There is an account from New York of two men of war and some tender got up beyond the city, — the Phœnix, Capt. Parker, and the Rose, Capt Wallace.

July 18, *Thursday*. — This day Independency was declared in Boston from the balcony of the Council Chamber; a great confusion in town.

July 20. — This morning advertisements were put up for the inhabitants to meet on Monday next at ten in the morning in the Common.

July 21, *Sunday*. — I went to church this morning. Mr. Parker omitted the petitions in the Liturgy for the King and royal family, thinking it prudent.

July 22–27. — [Visit, with Rev. Mr. Parker as companion, to Portsmouth, N. H., on business, — the division of some goods, perhaps brought in by a privateer, — dining with old Judge Parker and Mr. Jos. Wentworth in that town, and with Tristram Dalton at "Newberry Old Town." "We were smoaked at Charlestown, but passed at Newberry bridge."]

July 30. — [Capture of the ship Queen of England laden with provisions for General Howe's army, the ship belonging to Rowe's friend Jos. Squires of Plymouth.]

August 1. — This day is appointed by the Congress as a fast to be observed throughout the Colonies. I went to church this morning. Mr. Parker preached.

Aug. 3. — [A ship captured by privateers, laden with 400 hogsheads of sugar.]

Aug. 5. — Richard Green set out this morning for Brookfield for 4 months exile, James Perkins for 4 months to Medfield, Nat. Cary do. to Dedham, John Timmins and Thos. Amory two months to Waltham, William Perry 4 months to Medfield, and Nat. Brinly do. to Framingham.

Aug. 9. — [Captures by privateers.]

Aug. 11, *Sunday.* — After service Mr. Parker read the proclamation of Independence.

Aug. 14. — This day the Sons of Liberty kept the remembrance of it at John Marston's in King Street.

Aug. 15. — I dined at home with Genl. Lincoln, Elbridge Gerry, Esq., one of the delegates to the Congress, and Mrs. Rowe, and spent the evening at home with her.

Aug. 18, 19. — [Journey to Portsmouth for a law-suit, returning August 25. At Hampton " had the pleasure of the company of Mr. Ware, President of the Councill, who is a man of understanding."]

Aug. 21. — This morning our tryall came on. After dinner I attended the court. Our attorney, Mr. Loel [John Lowell], deserves praise, and is a gentleman of merit, and so is Mr Pickering [John Pickering, of Portsmouth], who pleaded as advocate for the captors and against us. They had not time to finish, and adjourned untill the morning. I spent the evening at Tilton's with my friends the other claimants, Saml. Austin, Robt. Ruggles, Nat. Barrat, Mr. Fraser, Mr. Cyrus Baldwin, Colo. Leveret, his son, and a young gentleman sent by our councill with the papers.

Aug. 22. — This morning our tryall came on again. The cause was given to the jury by Dr. Bracket, who is Judge of Admiralty. I dined at my worthy friend Mark Wentworth's, with him and his lady, my worthy friends Colo. Atkinson and Jonathan Warner, Esq., and Mr. King, a very sensible gentleman. This afternoon the jury brought in their verdict in our favour, viz., that the capture was not within the Act, and that the claimants ought to have their goods restored. This verdict is disliked by Capt. Manly, &c., and therefore he intends to move for an appeall. I spent the evening at Tilltons with Mr. Loell and our friends the claimants.

Aug. 23. — I with the rest of the claimants have tryed to settle this affair with the agent and Capt. Manly, but to no purpose. I slept at old Colo. Warner's last night and this, and had a long conversation with him and his lady, who I found to be a very sensible old gentleman.

Aug. 26. — Yesterday was our wedding day. We have been married thirty three years.

Aug. 28. — Mr. Saml. Adams and Colo. Whipple of Portsmouth came to town from Philadelphia this morning. The claimants met this forenoon; they chose a committee to report their cause to Saml. Adams, Esq., — myself, Mr. Saml. Austin, Capt. Saml. Partridge.

Aug. 31. — The post says that Generall Howe has landed some of his troops on Long Island near Flat Bush, and that some skirmishes had taken place.

Sept. 5. — I attended the Court of Admiralty in Boston, Judge Pickering. The Rev^d Mr. Payson paid me a visit. Severall skirmishes between the two armies at Long Island. Lord Sterling and Generall Sullivan are missing.

Sept. 7. — Tis said the Continentall troops have left Long Island.

Sept. 8, *Sunday.* — After church Colo. Langdon of Portsmouth paid me a visit. I spent the evening at home with Mr. Inman, Mrs. Inman, Mr. [Tristram] Dalton, and Mrs. Rowe. Several West India men carried into Providence by the Continental vessels.

Sept. 10. — I dined at Deacon Jones the Coffee House on turtle. Present Genl. Lincoln, Mr. Mercer [of New York], Mr. James Otis, Mr. Inman, myself, Dan! Johnnot, Geo. Johnnot, Jona. Amory, Henry Bromfield, his son, Colo. Barber, his son, Thos. Russell, young Williams, Capt. Job Prince, his son, Colo. Moore, Mr. Loell [Lowell], Mr. Sam. Brick, Mr. Hammat, Mr. Ross of Jamaica, Mr. Grant of the Grenady (?), Mr. Grant of Antigua, Mr. Cambell, Capt. Barthlet, Colo. Jackson, Mr. Warper, Jos. Laughton, Wm Vans, John Cushing, Benj. Andrews, Henderson Inches, Herman Brimmer, Martin Brimmer, And. Brimmer, Capt. John Bradford, Mr. Hastings, Capt. Thompson, Capt. White of Marblehead, Dr. Joseph Gardner, Major Ward, Major Wadsworth, Wm. Davis, Edward Davis, Mr. Elnathan Jones, Mr. Plat, Mr. Eben^r Storer, Capt. Pascall Smith, Mr. Ezekiel Price, Mr. Jos. Barrell, Mr. Burges, Mr. Lindall Pitts, and Jos. Carnes. We were very joyfull.

Sept. 14. — Tis said by the post, Mr. Mumpford, that the Continentalls have appointed three gentlemen from their body to hold conferences with Lord Howe and his brother Generall Howe, viz.: Benj. Franklynn, Esq., Philadelphia, Mr. Rutledge of South Carolina, and Mr. John Adams of Massachusetts Bay in New England, Braintree.

Sept. 17. — Yesterday the Independent Company made their appearance in the Common under the command of Colo. Jackson, and were reviewed by some of the Councill and Generall Ward and a number of other gentlemen.

Sept. 20, *Friday.* — The Continentall troops evacuated New York on Sunday last.

Sept. 21. — The post confirms the account of the army's evacuating the city of New York.

Aug. 26. — Gen¹ Hancock returned.

Aug. 28. — This morning the French fleet came to an anchor in Nantasket Road, some of them dismasted.

Aug. 29. — Some of d'Estaing's fleet came up into Boston harbour.

Aug. 30, *Sunday.* — The Count d'Estaing came with his retinue on shore yesterday, and dined with Genl. Hancock. Two frigates were seen in our bay this afternoon, supposed to be English.

Aug. 31. — An express from Plymouth this morning giving an account of a fleet of twenty sail in our bay this morning. [Arrival of prizes; Capt. Skimmer killed in an engagement with a letter of marque brig.]

Sept. 1. — The fleet appearing again in our bay has alarmed the people, that the whole of the militia are ordered under arms. Gen. Sullivan and his whole army have retired from Rhode Island, having had a smart engagement with the British troops there under the command of Gen¹ Piggot.

Sept. 2. — Severall people taken up and put on board the prize ship, particularly Mr. Shirley and Capt. Callahan. The militia under arms again twice this day, and a constant guard kept up. I met the Proprietors of Point Shirly this day. The French Admirall wants to be accommodated with the houses for an hospital for his people, upwards of 700 being sick of the scurvy.

Sept. 5. — Colo. Crafts came to town with his regiment this morning. We met them on the road [to Dedham].

Sept. 7. — Jack Rowe went to Chelsea this morning. The English have sent a party to [New] Bedford, and burnt it on Saturday night, together with the shipping and stores in that harbor.

Sept. 10. — I dined at home with the Honble Jery Powell, President of our Councill, and Mrs. Rowe.

Sept. 11. — High training this day. Gen. Hancock treated the Council and all his officers, many other gentlemen, at Capt. Marston's. The dinner was very clever. I dined there, and spent the evening at home with Capt. Haskins and Mrs. Rowe.

Sept. 13, *Sunday.* — The Rev. Dr. Elliot dyed this morning, much lamented.

Sept. 20, *Sunday.* — Mr. Parker preached a very serious and good sermon; he mentioned the character of that good and worthy man, the Rev. Dr. Elliot.

Sept. 22. — We have heard this day from George [Inman] and Sucky [Mrs. Linzee], who are well at New York.

Sept. 23. — Many prizes have arrived yesterday and this day in this harbour. The Count d'Estaing with his officers, &c., made a grand appearance yesterday; they paid a visit to the Generall Court, and were escorted by a committee of both Houses on their landing at the Long Wharff.

www.ingramcontent.com/pod-product-compliance
Lightning Source LLC
Chambersburg PA
CBHW071152140325
23506CB00012B/887